How to . . .

get the most from your
COLES NOTES

Key Point

Basic concepts in point form.

Close Up

Additional hints, notes, tips or background information.

Watch Out!

Areas where problems frequently occur.

Quick Tip

Concise ideas to help you learn what you need to know.

Remember This!

Essential material for mastery of the topic.

Your Guide to...

Beer

Canadian & world brews

Ales, lagers & others

Breweries —

major & micro

COLES NOTES have been an indispensable aid to students on five continents since 1948.

COLES NOTES now offer titles on a wide range of general interest topics as well as traditional academic subject areas and individual literary works. All COLES NOTES are written by experts in their fields and reviewed for accuracy by independent authorities and the Coles Editorial Board.

COLES NOTES provide clear, concise explanations of their subject areas. Proper use of COLES NOTES will result in a broader understanding of the topic being studied. For academic subjects, COLES NOTES are an invaluable aid for study, review and exam preparation. For literary works, COLES NOTES provide interesting interpretations and evaluations which supplement the text but are not intended as a substitute for reading the text itself. Use of the NOTES will serve not only to clarify the material being studied, but should enhance the reader's enjoyment of the topic.

© Copyright 2000 and Published by
COLES PUBLISHING. A division of Prospero Books
Toronto – Canada
Printed in Canada

Cataloguing in Publication Data
Wessell, Wayne 1944–

Your guide to ... beer : Canadian & world brews;
ales, lagers & others; breweries–major & micro

(Coles notes)
Written by Wayne Wessell.
Includes bibliographical references.
ISBN 0-7740-0614-5

1. Beer. 2. Ale. 3. Breweries. I. Title. II. Series.

TP577.W47 2000   641.2'3   C00-930778-8

Publisher: Nigel Berrisford
Editing: Paul Kropp Communications
Book design and layout: Karen Petherick, Markham, Ontario
Illustration: Christine Cullen

Manufactured by Webcom Limited
Cover finish: Webcom's Exclusive DURACOAT

Contents

CHAPTER ONE

Beer: An introduction

There are over 5000 breweries worldwide, which produce some 15,000 brands of beer. Is it any wonder that beer, after water, is the most popular beverage in the world?

The annual worldwide consumption of beer is approximately 134 billion litres – about 80 bottles a year for each person on the planet.

As late as the early 1980s, beer drinkers had few choices anywhere in North America. The only beer that we drank, for the most part, was a light-colored, fairly bland lager, a beer that is made in almost every country on earth. Today, those bland beers still exist and remain the most popular type, but since the mid-1980s a beer renaissance has been happening. The selection of beer now available to the Canadian consumer is absolutely mind-boggling. New breweries, new beers and new pubs seem to be arriving each day in our neighborhoods. The list of imported beers from all around the world is growing steadily and there are now hundreds of different beers available for us to enjoy.

Is it any wonder, then, that many beer drinkers only familiar with lager beer are amazed, confused and sometimes upset when they are confronted with a beer that might be darker, thicker or different-tasting from their traditional drink?

What are these different beers? What can you expect from them? Should you be bold and try something new, something exotic? This guide will help you make these choices and perhaps turn you into a beer aficionado, more adventurous in your beer selections.

1

CHOICES, CHOICES, CHOICES

Although there are almost 75 different styles of beer, there are only two beer types: ales and lagers. The differences between these two begin at brewing time.

Ales:

- are produced with top-fermenting yeast at warmer temperatures and ferment faster than lagers
- have been produced for thousands of years
- have a short aging period – from several days to a few weeks in a warm atmosphere
- are darker in color and heavier in body
- are more hoppy and less malty
- have less effervescence
- have a noticeable flavor that is more complex (fruity, bitter or a balance of both)
- are best served at 7° to 13°C

Lagers:

- are made with bottom-fermenting yeast at cooler temperatures and ferment more slowly than ales
- have only been made for the last 500 years; were not made with hops until the mid-1800s
- have a longer aging period – one to three months in cold storage (The word "lager" comes from the German *lagern*, which means "to store.")
- are lighter in color, clearer and lighter in body
- are less hoppy and more malty
- are more effervescent
- have a less pronounced flavor palate
- are best served at 10° to16°C

Beer characteristics

When describing a beer, many terms are used. Here are a few of them that will be useful in understanding the various beer styles.

Clarity	The degree of cloudiness in a beer, the result of the sediment in a bottle. Some beers, like unfiltered wheat beers, are meant to be cloudy. Lagers are not intended to be cloudy.
Color	The color of beer may range from very pale yellow to dark brown, almost black.
Effervescence	Highly carbonated beers like lagers, are said to be "crisp."
Body	The sensation of thickness in a beer. This can range from watery to creamy (or thin, medium or full-bodied).
Strength	Usually refers to the alcoholic content.
Hoppy	The taste comes from the flavors of the added hops. This is sometimes described as bitter, herbal, spicy or flowery.
Malty	The caramel flavors that result from the malted barley or other grains.
Roasty-toasty	The flavors produced from drying or kilning the malted grain. These can include caramel, chocolate, coffee and smokey.

ALE STYLES

While there are only two types of beer, the many styles within each type are quite different from each other.

Barley wine   Despite its name this is not a wine but a very strong beer. Usually with an alcoholic content of 7 to 10% alcohol by volume, barley wine is dark brown, fruity and bittersweet. It is normally served in a wine glass.

Belgian beers   A most unusual and complex group of ales. These beers are fully described in the section under Belgium and include Belgian ales, both pale and golden; Belgian strong ales; Flanders brown ales, Trappist or Abbey ales; Lambics, Saisons and Witbier.

Bière en garde   A spicy, heavily malted beer, traditionally made in the north of France.

Bitter   Originally, bitter was a term used to distinguish newly hopped beers from the old ales. Today bitter ale is highly hopped, dry, lightly carbonated and ranges in color from light gold to red. There are three subclasses of bitter: ordinary, best and extra special. The ordinary is the weakest and has the least amount of body, while the extra special has the most.

Brown ales   There are two types of brown ales: American and English.

American brown ale   Commonly called "nut brown ale," it is medium-bodied, smooth and hoppier than the English style. English brown ale has a sweet malt taste with very little hops.

Irish red ale   A sweet medium-bodied lightly hopped ale.

Old ale   A strong English ale that is malty-sweet, full-bodied and high in alcoholic content. It matures well and can be aged for several years.

Pale ales   Usually golden to amber in color, pale ales come in dry, fruity, nutty or toasty malt flavors. India pale ale is a beer that was developed in England for export to the British troops stationed abroad. It is hoppier than regular pale ale since the hops acted as a preservative for the long sea voyages.

Porter   A very dark, strong, full-bodied ale. Porter flavors are very complex, as the taste of the roasted malt gives a chocolate flavor that mingles with the bitterness of the hops. Originally developed in London by mixing light beer with heavier beer, porter was known as "entire." It was given the name "porter" because of its alleged popularity with the porters at Victoria Station in London.

Scottish ale   A full-bodied ale brewed in Scotland. It is less hoppy and maltier than the English ales.

Stout   Originally developed as a type of porter, stout is very full-bodied and almost black in color. There are several styles of stout – dry stout, oatmeal stout, sweet stout and Russian imperial stout.

Wheat beers   Made with as much as 60% wheat malt. These beers were originally made in Germany where they are known as Weizen or Weisse beers. There are several styles of wheat beers: Witbier, Weissbier, Hefeweizen, Dunkelweizen, Berliner Weisse and Weizenbock.

LAGER STYLES

American lagers   Most American lagers are light colored, somewhat watery, with a delicate sweetness. These are highly carbonated and have a balanced taste and aroma. Most are quite bland but refreshing when served very cold. Based on the classic Pilsner style, most American lagers taste very similar to each other. American brewers use a great amount of adjuncts (such as corn or rice) in the brewing of their beer. While the breweries claim that these adjuncts give a smoother beer, they also rob the brews of much of their flavor and aroma. The **light** version has almost no taste or aroma at all. Over 90% of all the beer consumed in the United States is this style of beer, regardless of its limitations.

Canadian lagers	Very much like the American lagers but with a little more body, Canadian beers were always thought to be stronger than American brews because they have more body and flavor. But there is really very little difference in the beers from these two countries. Almost all Canadian beers are 5% alcohol by volume (ABV). Most American beers are 4.5 to 4.8% ABV. Virtually every country that brews beer has a brewery making a lager that is similar in taste and style.
Bock beers	These beers are traditionally very dark and full-bodied. These are quite malty with chocolate undertones. There are several styles of bock beer: traditional bock, double bock, triple bock, maibock (a light-colored bock) and eisbock.
Dry beer	The idea of dry beer is to remove any aftertaste or finish in the beer. As a result dry beer has very little flavor, so little that you don't even realize that you are drinking a beer. The product originated in Japan and eventually spread all over the world, perhaps consumed by those people who don't really like the taste of beer.
Dortmunder	The traditional lager or Pilsner of the city of Dortmund, Germany. It has a distinctive flowery aroma, is medium- to full-bodied and pale gold in color. Dortmunder is not as hoppy and is much sweeter than traditional Pilsner.
Helles or Munchener Helles	The pale lager of Munich, Germany. The beer is very malty and lightly hopped. It is the regular beer served in the beerhalls of Munich.
Marzen or Oktoberfest beer	An amber or copper-colored beer that was traditionally brewed for the autumn harvest-time. Marzen is quite similar to bock beer but without the chocolate flavor.
Pilsner	The original Pilsner lager was brewed in Pilzen (Pilsen), Bohemia, now part of the Czech Republic. All other brewers of lager around the world based

their styles on this original. Czech Pilsners are slightly malty, aromatic and hoppy with a dry finish. Only Czech Pilsners may use this spelling. Other Pilsner-type beers must use Pilsener or Pils on their labels. German Pilseners or Pils are lighter, hoppier and less malty than their Czech cousins.

Vienna-style lager   An amber-red lager that was first brewed in Austria, it is very similar to Marzen. Vienna lager has a sweet malty taste balanced by a mild hop bitterness.

HYBRIDS

Some beers don't fit into either the ale or lager categories. They are called hybrids because the brewers mix up the way that they are brewed, fermented or aged.

Alt   In German "alt" means old and in this case, it means brewed in the old way. Alt beers are fermented warm with top-fermenting yeast, like ales, but aged in a cool place, like lagers. Alt beer is a darker color, anywhere from copper brown to dark brown. It is usually quite bitter and malty.

Steam beer (California common beer)   A truly American-style beer, steam beer is said to have been developed in San Francisco during the gold rush days of the mid-1800s A hybrid of ale and lager brewing, it is fermented with bottom-fermenting (lager-style) yeast but at a warmer temperature. This is because ice or cold storage, essential for lager aging, wasn't available in the 1800s. The brewers then pumped the warm beer into kegs where it continued to ferment and produce its own natural carbonation. When the kegs were tapped, the excess carbonation hissed out like steam, giving the beer style its own name.

Cream ale   Another American invention produced when the brewers mixed bottom-fermenting yeast with top-fermenting yeast. The resulting beer is very light, smooth and low-in-hop flavor and aroma.

Kolsch   This is a beer that is made only in the city of Koln

(Cologne). An Alt-style beer, it is blonde in color and a little bitter in taste. Normally it is unfiltered and cloudy in appearance.

SPECIALTY BREWS

These are beers that are brewed in the regular way but use an adjunct (additive) to give the brew a special flavor.

Fruit and vegetable beers	These are usually ales that have been given natural flavors by adding real fruit or vegetables. Examples include beers made with cherry, apricot, raspberry, blueberry or pumpkin.
Herb and spice beers	Common spices used are cinnamon, anise (licorice), cloves, ginger, nutmeg, fennel or coriander. These beers are usually made as special holiday drinks.
Smoked beers	Any beer style can be smoked. German Rauchbiers are probably the most famous of the smoked beers.

CHAPTER TWO

A history of beer

No one is sure when the first beer was brewed, but as far as records go, there are references to brewing dating back over 6000 years. Actually the brewing recipe is quite simple: take some barley, add water, heat, a little yeast and presto – beer!

It's likely that some anonymous people put some cereal grain in water and heated it with the intention of softening it to eat it. They drew off the water and set it aside. Some airborne yeast happened to land in the water causing fermentation and by accident, a new drink is introduced to the world.

Historians have traced the roots of brewing back to many ancient civilizations, including Africans, Babylonians, Chinese, Egyptians, Incas, Sumarians and Hebrews. All made a coarse form of beer using whatever cereal grains were available. Beer was considered to be part of their essential diet, providing many of the fundamental nutrients for daily living. It was also considered to be a potion to ward off certain illnesses, especially when combined with certain herbs.

Ancient people often drank out of a communal vat of beer. This beer would hardly resemble the beer of today. It was probably more like a thin, sour porridge with a bit of a kick. The villagers would sit around this vat telling stories and drinking the brew out of long straws used to penetrate the surface scum and reach the clear brew at the bottom of the vat. In wealthy Egypt, it was recorded that the nobles used straws of gold in their beer drinking.

BEER'S DEVELOPMENT THROUGH THE AGES

6000 BC Babylonian artifacts found in ancient Iran have been identified by archeologists as the first remnants of beer making. This discovery suggests that the craft of brewing beer was known over 8000 years ago. Historians calculate that half of the Babylonian's grain harvest was used for making beer.

2500 BC In Egypt, hieroglyphics were found that show the Egyptians carrying out the full process of beer brewing. This procedure involved baking bread and crumbling it into water, then storing the mixture in earthenware jars. The Egyptians made a great variety of beers, which were available to everyone – nobles and peasants alike. Tax debts were often paid off with jars of beer. Even the laborers who built the pyramids were given daily stipends of beer. The Egyptians called their beer *hek*. The drink was so popular and hek-houses were so numerous that the authorities tried to ban the consumption of this beverage in 2000 BC, creating the first recorded instance of prohibition.

2000 BC Clay tablets, discovered by archeologists in the region previously known as Assyria, list beer as one of the food items taken aboard the ark by Noah. (Did he take two vats and two straws?)

1200 BC Jews in the Old Testament made a drink they called *sciera*, which was made from barley. It is likely that this was simply the recipe for *hek* brought out of Egypt during the Exodus.

800 BC Phoenician trading ships travelling north out of the Mediterranean introduced barley and beer to Northern Europe.

1300 Marco Polo wrote in his manuscripts about *kiu*, a beer that the Chinese had been making for a thousand years.

1500 In 1516, Wilhelm IV of Bavaria decreed that only the natural ingredients of malt (malted barley or wheat), hops, yeast and water could be used in the brewing of beer in Bavaria. The law strictly stated that no additives, such as sugar, rice or corn, were allowed in the production of beer. This law was known as "Reinheitsgebot," the German pure beer law, a policy still followed today in all of Germany and in many other parts of the world. Brewers who disobeyed were often thrown in jail.

Many beers brewed today have on their labels a statement such as "our beer is handcrafted to conform with the Bavarian Reinheitsgebot purity laws enacted in 1516, using only the finest malted barley or wheat, hops, water and yeast." This is important only because many of the large corporate brewers are famous for using cheaper ingredients such as corn or rice instead of malted barley or wheat.

Louis Pasteur

This great French scientist, after whom pasteurization was named, wrote *Etudes sur le Bière* in 1876. This work was a study of fermentation, the diseases of beer and the ways to prevent them. Pasteur was the first to establish the scientific role of yeast in the fermentation process. Pasteur's opus was dedicated to improving French beer. Although his countrymen ignored his scientific findings, the British and the Germans took it to heart and made immense improvements in their brewing operations.

In 1890 Emil Christian Hansen, a Danish brewer from the Carlsberg Brewery in Copenhagen, expanded on Pasteur's ideas. Hansen developed a procedure for isolating and cultivating yeast, a process worked to ensure brewing consistency by eliminating bad yeast strains.

Brewsters

From the earliest times women have been the brewers of beer. These brewers or brewsters, as they were called, produced beer at home for both their own family's consumption and for sale to their neighbors. Within their towns and villages, brewsters were held in very high regard.

Beer was believed to be a gift from the goddesses and it was customary for a brewster to offer a small amount from each beer batch to her beer goddess as a sacrifice.

Women continued to dominate as brewers until the 1880s. In Old England they were called alewives and often wore bright red caps. The term "mother red cap" was an expression used to describe them. There were many tales of dishonest alewives who fleeced their intoxicated customers by serving them watered down beer or by giving them short measures. Severe penalties were handed out to those who were caught selling poor beer.

As the church became more involved in the brewing process, making beer in the monasteries in large quantities and selling it in the inns they controlled, women brewers became less important and men began to control the brewing industry.

BEER IN THE BRITISH ISLES

When the Romans arrived in Britain, they discovered tribes who produced their own primitive brew from the natural products of the land. The Romans disliked the Celtic brews, which they considered to be undrinkable, and stuck to their wine and mead. The Vikings, many of whom were natives of Denmark, introduced true ale into Britain. The Danes brewed a drink they called *öl*, a name that evolved into "ale." This term became the name for all of the brews made in Northern Europe.

The original beer of the Celts would be unrecognizable to today's beer drinkers. It was dark, cloudy and had a heavy malt taste, lacking the "beer taste" we associate with modern beers. Seasonings such as berries, spices, leaves and, eventually, hops were added. Hops had been used in beer production since the eighth century but it wasn't until later that the use of hops to flavor beer became widespread.

For hundreds of years, ale was the beverage of Britain. People from all levels of society drank it: kings, queens, knights, abbots, monks and commoners. There were no large breweries, just a local brewer in each town or village who grew his own barley while his wife, the brewster, did the brewing. Brewers in this time were under heavy public and manorial scrutiny. Those who brewed "bad beer" were sometimes punished for their inferior product with a dunking on the village-dunking stool.

In the 1400s, patrons would be invited by the brewer to his alehouse in order to sample the brew. Attention was drawn to his establishment by placing a pole or a broom above the brewer's door. This was the first inn sign. People began to look for a pole hanging above the door that indicated this was a place where people gathered to drink and socialize – the pub was born! By the late 1400s England required that the pole, now called an ale-stake, be removed when no ale was available.

British folktales tell of Robin Hood and his merry men drinking ale and many of the alehouses adopted the legend of Robin and his men as native heroes:

> *To gentlemen and yeomen good*
> *Come in and drink with Robin Hood.*
> *If Robin Hood is not at home*
> *Come in and drink with Little John.*
> – Anonymous pub sign

Brewing with hops was popular in Europe in the fifteenth century and soon English brewers also began using hops in their brews. This improvement was met with indifference from the British public. Many thought that they might be poisoned by the bitter hops, which took away the malty sweetness found in their traditional ales. Various writers took up the cause and condemned the new drink as a health hazard. Even Henry VIII, perhaps under pressure from the local ale producers, decreed that the Royal Brewer in 1530 was not to use hops in his brews. With such terrible warnings, it is not surprising that it took many years for the new drink to become firmly established. By the late 1600s, however, hopped beer, which was a much smoother drink, had become the national drink.

Britain in the eighteenth century saw the great struggle between gin and beer. Both were made from grains – one distilled, the other brewed. Gin was the far stronger drink and it was cheaper. As a quarter of Britain's public houses became gin shops, gin became the bane of the working class. Beer, on the other hand, was depicted as the saviour of mankind:

> *Gin! Cursed friend with fury fraught*
> *Makes human race a prey.*
> *It enters by a deadly draught*
> *And steals our heart away.*
> *Beer! Happy produce of our isle*
> *Can sinewy strength impart,*
> *And, wearied with fatigue and toil,*
> *Can cheer each manly heart.*

The all-time record for drinking beer is believed to be held by an eighteenth century fellow named Jedediah Burton, who kept a record of all of the free beers that he had accepted since the age of 12. This amounted to 5115 pints or "winds" as he called them. Jedediah coined this term because it took him one wind or breath to drink one.

By the mid-nineteenth century the six major brewers in Britain had established themselves:

1666 – Trumans in London
1749 – Youngers in Scotland
1750 – Whitbread's in London
1750 – Guinness in Dublin
1787 – John Courage in England
1850 – Watneys in England

All of these breweries produced the traditional ales and porters of the day, usually of the unhopped variety. By 1870 there were 133,840 smaller breweries in Great Britain, private or local breweries producing beer in small amounts for local consumption.

Over the next 20 years the number of small breweries greatly diminished as new laws controlling the production of beer were passed. By 1906 there were only 1418 breweries left. Many of the smaller brewers had been bought out by the bigger breweries increasing their size and wealth. The practice of buying out smaller breweries and merging continued through the 1960s until there were only a handful of brewers making beer for all of Britain. Most of the beer produced had little character as the megabrewers called the Big Six (Bass, Allied, Whitbread, Watney, Courage, and Scottish and Newcastle) preferred to make keg beers that somehow had lost the distinctive "British flavor." This provided the impetus for the birth of CAMRA.

The Campaign for Real Ale (CAMRA), started in 1971 by a group of people concerned about the quality of British beer, initiated steps to save what they called "real ale." The original organizers did not realize that they would be creating a national consumer movement. Almost immediately thousands of people jumped on the bandwagon, expressing their dissatisfaction for the beer brewed by the big breweries. As a result, public awareness of the difference between cask-conditioned ale (real ale) and the beer being pushed by the big breweries increased dramatically. Soon consumers were demanding a different taste and the response was met. Since the mid-1970s hundreds of microbreweries have opened, offering a wonderful variety of real ales. Even the big breweries have bought into the idea by purchasing small breweries and producing real ales themselves. CAMRA now publishes the *Good Pub Guide*, an annual publication that identifies the pubs that serve the best real ales.

HERE COMES THE LAGER

The simple addition of hops to the brew did not instantly create lager as we know it. As far back as 700 AD brewers were adding hops to improve the taste of their brews. By the fifteenth century brewers in Bavaria learned to make beers by "lagering" a term derived from the German *lagern* – "to store." They had found that summer brewing often created "sour beer," caused by wild yeast in the air. Brewers then discovered yeast that would sink to the bottom of the brewing vats, thus becoming the first to produce bottom-fermenting beers, which we now call lagers. The brewers also observed that their beer was less susceptible to souring when it was stored in icy Alpine caves during the summer. This observation led them to seek colder fermentation periods followed by several months of aging in very cold conditions. This process resulted in a new light-colored beer that was quite mellow and refreshing. The popularity of this new lager swept across Europe and around the world.

In the 1850s a brand new lager from Bohemia appeared called Pilsner after the place of its origin, Pilzen. Legend has it that a strain of the bottom-fermenting yeast developed in Bavaria was stolen and smuggled to a Bohemian brewer. This yeast, when combined with Bohemian hops and local water, produced an amazing beer. Pilsner Urquell (the "original Pilsner") was then shipped all over the world. Brewers worldwide began to copy this new Pilsner and many of the most popular beers in the world have descended from these original Bohemian beers. In fact, lager has become the most popular style of beer throughout the world. Only in Britain and in Belgium has ale remained the prevalent beverage.

BREWING IN CANADA

The earliest recorded brewery in Canada was built in 1668 by Jean Talon, the Intendant of New France. Talon's aim was to encourage the colonists, who were dependent on wine and beer imported from France, to become more self-sufficient. But Talon returned to France in 1675, the brewery closed down and the colonists returned to their imported drink.

Over the next 100 years, many small breweries existed in both Upper and Lower Canada but these served only their local communities and their products were inconsistent in quality. The colonists continued to rely on the ale and porter from England, which often sold for more than the rum imported from the Caribbean. Not surprisingly, when John Molson opened his brewery in 1786, the Montreal beer drinkers welcomed him with open arms.

THE BIG TWO

For many years the Canadian beer market was dominated by three megabrewers: Molson's, Carling-O'Keefe and Labatt's. Recently Molson's purchased Carling-O'Keefe to reduce the number to two. Thus about 95% of all the beer brewed in Canada is produced by these two companies, now known as the "Big Two."

Molson Breweries (Les Brasseries Molson) John Molson arrived in Montreal in 1782 with a copy of John Richardson's *Theoretical Hints on an Improved Practice of Brewing* and within four years opened a brewery down by the St. Lawrence River. Molson's (the oldest brewery in North America) stands on the site of the original. The John Molson Company is also Canada's second oldest business, after the Hudson's Bay Company. The brewery became very successful and laid the foundation upon which Molson built an empire that included Canada's first railway and the Molson Bank, which became Bank of Montreal.

The Molson family tried to break into the Ontario market as early as 1850, but was thwarted in obtaining a permit to build a brewery when local politicians sought to protect their businesses. Instead the company continued its expansion by buying up smaller breweries. More than 40 breweries were acquired to contribute to the makeup of the present-day Molson's. The last acquisition was Carling-O'Keefe.

Carling-O'Keefe The second important Canadian brewer was Eugene O'Keefe who started brewing beer in 1862. He eventually built a new brewery in Toronto that specialized in the new lager style that was sweeping the world. O'Keefe eventually merged with the Carling Brewery, which had been established by Thomas Carling in 1840. Their newly established company soon became the largest brewery in Canada and later owned brewing operations in the United States and England.

After prohibition, E.P. Taylor, who had bought the Bradings Brewing company, started to acquire other breweries in Canada. By 1930 his firm had purchased nine, including Carling-O'Keefe. E.P.'s company, Canadian Breweries, was bought out by Rothman's in 1969 and renamed Carling-O'Keefe. Then in 1987 it was purchased by the

Foster Brewing Company of Australia. Finally, in 1989 Foster's joined Molson's and Carling-O'Keefe to form one part of the Big Two.

Labatt Brewery The John Labatt Brewery was founded by farmer John Labatt in 1847 outside of London, Ontario, when Labatt and his partner Samuel Eccles purchased a local brewery. Within six years Labatt assumed full control of the establishment, renaming the brewery the John Labatt Brewery. This brewery expanded as Canada grew and soon Labatt had breweries all across the country as John Labatt Jr. took over the company. During Prohibition, the brewery survived by making 2.5% beer for the domestic market and full strength beer for export. In the 1940s and '50s Labatt's also bought out breweries across the nation, allowing them to eventually set up breweries in almost every province.

In 1951, Labatt's brought out their new Pilsner, a beer that would soon be simply known as Blue and that would become by the 1990s Canada's number-one selling beer. Labatt's would also expand internationally purchasing the Morrelli Brewery in Italy and the Latrobe Brewing Company in Pennsylvania, which brews Rolling Rock. Recently Labatt's itself was bought by the giant Belgium company Interbrew.

There are three other historical breweries that should be mentioned:

Northern Breweries, Sault Ste. Marie Northern Breweries is made up of three separate breweries that date back to the early twentieth century. In 1960 the breweries were joined together to form the Doran Northern Brewing Company. In 1971 Canadian Breweries, which at that time was in the business of acquiring as many breweries as possible, took over. In 1977 Carling-O'Keefe, which replaced Canadian Brewers, sold the Doran Northern Group to the employees and Northern became the only worker-owned brewery in North America at the time.

Sleeman Brewing Company Sleeman's has an interesting history as a tale of two John Sleeman's: First John Sleeman opened a brewery in St. Catharines in 1837 and continued to operate up until Prohibition in Canada. Then John Sleeman, grandson of the original family brewer, came along with his grandfather's recipe book in hand and reopened the Sleeman Brewery, this time in Guelph, in 1987.

Moosehead Breweries John and Susannah Oland began brewing beer in Nova Scotia, in 1867. The brewery grew steadily with Susannah running it herself for 17 years. Unfortunately the brewery was completely destroyed in the Halifax explosion of 1917. After that the family split, with each group opening their own breweries. In 1928, the one in Halifax became the Oland Brewery, and the one in New Brunswick became Moosehead Breweries. The Oland operation eventually sold out to Labatt's in 1971, leaving Moosehead as the only local Maritimes brewer. Soon Moosehead was exporting its beer to the United States and Great Britain, but not the rest of Canada. Until 1992 odd licensing law prevented Moosehead from shipping to other provinces. Thankfully those laws have since been repealed, and the rest of Canada can now enjoy Moosehead.

BREWING IN THE UNITED STATES

In America, indigenous peoples were brewing their beer long before Christopher Columbus arrived. Tribes living in what is now the South West United States made a beer very similar to that produced by both the Aztecs of Mexico and the Incas of Peru. The Spanish referred to this beer as *chicha*, since it was corn based. This drink was a communal beverage produced by the women who chewed the corn, spat it into a large bowl and allowed the mixture to ferment for several days. The whole tribe, probably through reed straws, then consumed the *chicha*.

More traditional beer came to America aboard the *Mayflower*, which brought casks of ale as part of its manifest. This "beere" was considered to be essential to the health of the colonists. It has even been suggested that the *Mayflower* landed at Plymouth Rock rather than continuing on to its destination of Virginia for lack of beer. "We could not now take time for further search or consideration, our victuals being much spent, especially our beere."

Several breweries were established in Virginia in the early 1700s. These early brewers used corn or maize rather than barley, and the beer was unhopped, much like the early beer made in England. But for the most part, the American settlers relied on shipments of beer from England. The colonists felt that beer was far more healthful than the questionable water sources available to them and were quick to found these local breweries as a means of supplementing their supplies from England. (Breweries in the New World were among the first businesses established in America, pre-existing the American government.)

In 1587 Virginia, Sir Walter Raleigh founded the first brewery in America. Fifty-five years later in 1632, the first major brewery, the Netherlands West India Company Brewery, was begun in New Amsterdam (New York) by Dutch settlers. Scores of Dutch breweries followed in the same area on Brouwer Straat (Brewer's Street), not far from the East River. In 1683, William Penn, the founder of Pennsylvania, started a brewery on his estate outside of Philadelphia.

The beer produced in these colonial times came from the breweries in barrels or casks. This draught beer (later shortened to draft) was drunk from black leather containers or jugs called "black jacks." Later in the 1600s, pewter tankards were used. But it wasn't until the 1700s that the beer drinker could enjoy his favorite beverage from a glass. Bottled beer had been imported on rare occasions; it wasn't until after 1760 that domestic brews were bottled, and not until the next century that the American glass industry could support beer bottling on a wide scale.

Many famous American patriots, including George Washington, Samuel Adams, Thomas Jefferson, Benjamin Franklin and James Madison, were well-known brewers. In fact, these men were not only opposed to the heavy taxation imposed by the English but also to the importation of English beers. In 1770, they were vocal in recommending the boycott of these imports in favor of the locally brewed beers.

By 1840 about 140 breweries were operating in the United States, at least one in each of the 13 original colonies. Around this time America's taste for beer changed as more and more immigrants from Northern Europe arrived, bringing with them their knowledge of brewing and a preference for something other than British ale and porter.

It was at this time that a Bavarian brewer named Johann Wagner arrived in Philadelphia (1841), bringing a new yeast and a recipe for a bottom-fermenting beer called lager. The lager revolution that had swept Europe a few years earlier now swept the United States. More and more settlers arrived from Germany, setting up new brewing operations and changing the face of American brewing forever.

Probably no place is better identified with beer than Milwaukee, Wisconsin. Nearly 75 different brewers have come and gone but Milwaukee is best remembered for the four giant breweries that turned this town into America's beer capital. These brewers were Joseph Schlitz, Frederic Miller, Valentin Blatz and Frederick Pabst. The Joseph Schlitz Brewing Company started in 1858, brewing "the beer that made Milwaukee famous." It was eventually bought out in 1982 by Stroh's of Detroit. Former Great Lakes steamship captain, Pabst took over the Empire Brewery in 1889, renaming it the Pabst, Brewing Company. In 1853 Miller took over the Plank Road Brewery. Miller's eventually became the world's second largest brewery. Meanwhile in 1852, Anheuser-Busch, the brewer of Budweiser began its operations in St. Louis. It is now the largest brewer in the world, producing over 800 million barrels of beer annually.

Some interesting dates
in beer history

1251 King Gambrinus, known as the "patron saint of beer" or the "king of beers" has been a symbol of beer and brewing in Northern Europe. Some credit him with the invention of hopped malt beer and with the introduction of the toast as a social custom.

1759 Guinness opens the St. James Gate Brewery in Dublin, Ireland.

1772 A new beverage called porter is brewed in London, England, as an alternative to the malty ales.

1777 Bass, now Britain's largest brewing conglomerate, is founded in Burton-on-Trent because of the quality of the local water.

1789 John Molson founds his brewery in Montreal. It is the oldest brewery in North America.

1847 John Labatt begins brewing beer in London, Ontario.

1852 Anheuser-Busch, brewer of Budweiser, begins in St. Louis, the first step on their way to becoming the world's largest brewer.

1874 Carlsberg, one the most famous breweries in the world is started by Jacob Christian Jacobsen. The first part of the brewery name came from his son, Carl. The second part is from the term "berg" or the hill on which the brewery stood.

1920 Prohibition stops the production and sale of alcoholic drinks everywhere in the United States and Canada, except for Quebec, which allowed beer and wine.

1935 The first beer can is introduced by the Kreuger Beer Co. of New Jersey.

1951 Labatt's brings out their new Pilsner Lager Beer, a beer that would eventually be called "Blue" and become Canada's best-selling beer.

1959 Coors introduces the lighter, more practical aluminum can.

1971 CAMRA the Campaign for Real Ale, is started in Britain.

1978 Light beer is brought onto the Canadian market and within 10 years it represents 20% of beer sales.

1989 The "Big Three" become the "Big Two" as Molson's takes over Carling-O'Keefe.

CHAPTER THREE

How beer is made

The brewing process is a fairly simple procedure that has been reproduced for hundreds of years. The only difference today is the use of modern equipment that all but eliminates the possibility of a "bad brew."

All brewers follow the same basic steps in the brewing process:

Step 1: Malting

The malting process involves getting the barley ready for brewing. It is designed to unlock the starches and enzymes in the barley, allowing them to be useful in the brewing process. Malting consists of three stages:

Steeping: The barley is soaked in water for about 40 hours to increase the water content of the grain.

Germination: The soaked barley is spread out on the floor where it is allowed to germinate (grow little seedlings). This stage lasts about five days until hot air is blown over the barley, stopping the germination process. Malted barley is now formed but it must be dried.

Kilning: The malt is then transferred to a kiln where it is roasted. The roasting time and temperature depend on the type of malt needed by the brewer. Some malts will end up quite pale in color, others will get very dark. Roasting the malt creates the various colors and tastes in beer.

Step 2: Milling

At this point the malted barley is brought to the brewing house and fed into the grain. Milling is the cracking or crushing of the

23

kernels of malted grain. This will allow the grain to absorb water in order to extract sugars from the malt.

Step 3: Mashing

The crushed grain, now called grist, is fed into a large container, named the mash tun, and mixed with warm water. A porridge-like cereal mash is soon formed and the starches in the tun are slowly converted to sugars.

In some systems, a second container, called a lauter tun, is used. Here the mash is held in the vessel for a period of time and then strained through the bottom of the lauter tun.

The resulting sugary liquid is called the wort or sweet liquor. The leftover or spent grain in the mash is then sold to farmers for cattle feed.

Step 4: Brewing

The wort passes into the brew kettle where it is boiled for one to two hours. Traditionally these brewing vessels were made of copper and were often called coppers. At this time the brewer may add or pitch the hops into the wort.

The timing of the addition of hops is significant: early pitching imparts bitterness to the brew; adding the hops later in the boil gives the brew its flavor and aroma.

The hops are then strained out of the wort as it passes through the hop jack. The remaining wort is sent to a whirlpool to remove any bits of hops or grain still remaining, as these bits could give the beer a harsh taste. The whirlpool also removes any proteins that could give the beer a cloudy appearance or haze.

Scotch and beer

The process of making Scotch whisky is very similar to that of making beer. Both processes use malted barley, which gets mashed, milled, boiled and fermented. But malt whisky does not use hops, and after fermentation it is distilled. Nevertheless both beer and Scotch whisky do share the scent of malt.

Step 5: Cooling

Next the wort is passed into a heat exchanger or wort chiller where it is quickly cooled down. The wort must be cooled to a point where yeast can be safely added. Since yeast will not grow or ferment at high temperatures, the brewer must wait until the temperature is below 20°C.

Step 6: Fermenting

The wort is pumped into the fermentation tank. Here yeast is added or pitched into the tank. This pitching must be done when the wort is at the correct temperature. For ales it should be 12° to 18°C; for lagers it should be 6° to 12°C. As the yeast ferments, it turns the wort sugars into alcohol. This process may take five to 10 days, depending on the style of beer being brewed.

Step 7: Aging

The liquid is now transferred to the aging tanks. Sometimes the brewer will allow a secondary fermentation to occur in these tanks. Aging is intended to improve the flavor and taste of the beer, although this doesn't take very long. Ales will usually mature within a few weeks while lagers may take several months (usually at a much colder temperature).

Kraeusen brewing

Sometimes the brewer may use an old German technique to condition (age) the beer. This method is called Kraeusening (or Krausening). The brewer adds a small amount of young fermenting wort to the fully fermented one, producing a secondary fermentation. The beer is then sealed and carbon dioxide, produced by this secondary fermentation, is allowed to build up. This process conditions the beer. A clarifying agent is then added to settle the yeast. Early brewers used beechwood chips for this process.

Step 8: Finishing

After the beer has been aged, it is filtered several times to remove any remaining yeast.

The beer is then packaged in bottles, cans or kegs. Most bottled or canned beer is pasteurized before it is packaged.

Step 9: Sampling

A typical brewery

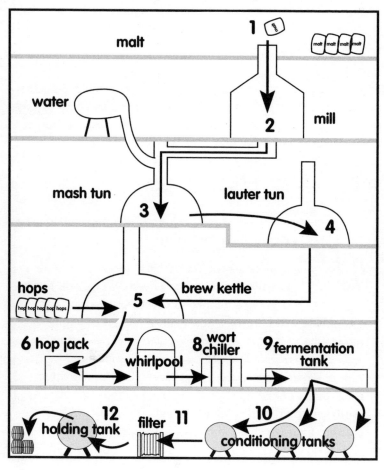

INGREDIENTS

The different ingredients in beer result in different styles and flavors in the finished product. Here are some of the more important ones.

Water

Water can have a great effect in the production of beer. Some of the classic beers get their unique taste from the water used to make them. Several of the legendary British ales, such as Bass, are made in Burton-on-Trent, in the English Midlands. Here the local water has a high content of calcium and magnesium. This aids the action of the hops during the brewing process. Many modern brewers elsewhere will harden their water by adding Burton salts to make this particular style of beer. The famous Pilsner beers of Bohemia, such as Pilsner Urquell, are made with a very soft water found in the ground near the breweries.

Brewers have a choice when brewing whether to use local municipal water or water from a spring or well. The advantage of using spring or well water is that it might contain certain salts that benefit some types of beer making. The brewer has to know how the water being used will react with the other brewing materials, the malted barley, yeast and hops. Today brewers will change the water that they are using to suit the beer being made. Here are some of the key components they consider:

Calcium	Makes water hard and is important in mashing and brewing.
Magnesium	Is a secondary source of hardness and a yeast nutrient.
Sodium chloride	Gives the beer a sour or salty taste that can change the flavor of the beer.
Iron	Gives a metallic flavor and is usually undesirable.
Carbonate (Bicarbonate)	Affects the pH of the water by changing its alkalinity, thus changing the taste of the beer.
Sulphate	Alters the flavor producing a drier, sharper taste, sometimes a bitter taste.
Chloride	Changes the beer flavor. It can affect the stability and improve clarity.

You have seen those ads for beer claiming to be made with water from "mountain-fed springs." Breweries are likely to brag about their water source if it is decidedly different from normal tap water, but the most important factor is that it be good drinking water.

Barley

Barley is the most commonly used grain in the art of brewing. A member of the grass family, barley is grown in two forms, two-row and six-row so called because of the number of rows of barley kernels on the stalk. Generally, two-row barley is used for brewing ales and six-row for making lagers. Some breweries don't necessarily follow this pattern. Molson's, for example, claims to use 100% two-row barley in all of their brews.

To be of any use in the brewing process, barley must first be malted. Without malting, the grain cannot be fermented. Its starches must be broken down into usable sugars that can be converted to alcohol. Malted barley comes in a variety of colors, flavors and degrees of roastedness. These differences give beer its color, malty sweet flavor and body. In addition, the enzymes found in the malt are needed to aid in fermentation.

Here are some of the commonly used malts:

Lager malt   Cooked at fairly low temperatures, it is the lightest in color of all the malts; used in the production of Pilsners, lagers and some pale ales.

Pale ale malt   Cooked a little longer for a darker color, it is used for pale ales and English bitters.

Wheat malt   Quite light in color, it is used only for wheat-style beers.

Mild ale malt   Kilned at higher temperatures for a caramel color, this beer takes on a stronger toffee-like flavor. Used for mild ales and Vienna-style lagers.

Crystal malt   Cooked at fast-rising temperatures for a reddish color and sweet flavor. Used for bock beers and amber lagers.

Chocolate malt Roasted at very high temperatures for a very dark chocolate-brown color. The flavor may be like coffee or burnt chocolate. Used for stouts, porters and brown ales.

Black malt Kilned for a longer time, it is roasted to a very dark, almost black color. It gives the dark color and bite to stouts.

Hops

The hops used in the brewing process are small pine cone-like flowers that grow on the hops plant. The plant grows like a vine, often as tall as 7.5 m (25 ft.). The flowers are often hand-picked because they are so delicate and are easily damaged, spoiling their characteristics. The cone or flower is yellowish-green and can be up to 10 cm (4 in.) long. Small glands called lupulin glands contain resins and oils that provide the bitterness, flavor and aroma of the hops.

As far back as the eighth century, hops were being used along with other ingredients such as berries, leaves, tree bark, flowers and various spices to help tone down the sweet maltiness of ale. By the sixteenth century hops had become the most commonly used spice for the bittering of beer.

Hops are used to:

- add a bitter flavor
- give a pungent aroma
- balance out the malty sweetness
- aid in preserving the beer by extending its shelf life

There are more than 50 varieties of hops, each with its own distinctive flavor and aroma. Some are considered better for bittering, others for their aromatic qualities.

Brewers will usually categorize their hops into three categories: copper hops, late hops and dry hops.

Copper hops are bittering hops used in the boiler (boilers used to all be made of copper). These hops are high in alpha acid, the bittering agent, giving the beer its distinctive bitter taste.

Late hops are added later in the boil, usually in the last five to 15 minutes. These hops give the beer much of its aroma and flavor.

Dry hops may be put into the primary fermentation, the secondary fermentation or directly into the cask just after filling.

These will add additional aromatic qualities to the beer. The brewer tries to balance the flavor and the aroma of the beer to give the beer its own distinctive character.

Some varieties of hops:

Brewer's Gold	A bittering hop for ales.
Cascade	Provides both aroma and bittering for ales.
Fuggles	A traditional ale aroma hop.
Golding	A traditional ale aroma hop.
Hallentauer	A traditional all-purpose German lager hop.
Mt. Hood	Commonly used in American lagers.
Northern Brewer	Used for both ales and lagers – multi-purpose.
Saaz	The traditional hop used in Pilsner beers.

Yeast

Yeast is responsible for carrying out the fermentation process that produces the alcohol in beer. Most beers contain between 4 and 5% alcohol by volume. The true role of yeast was not discovered until Louis Pasteur published his ideas on how yeast affected the brewing process. In fact, the German Purity Act (the Reinheitsgebot) of 1537 does not mention yeast because brewers were not aware of its importance. It wasn't until the eighteenth century that a distinction between ale and lager yeast was developed.

Ale yeast stays on top of the brew, now called top-fermented beer. It works best in warmer temperatures: 15° to 24°C.

Lager yeast goes to the bottom of the brew and works best at colder temperatures: 3° to 11°C.

The most commonly used yeasts are species of the genus *Saccharomyces*. Ale yeasts are called *cerevisiae* and lager yeasts, *carlsbergensis*. The lager yeast is named after the Carlsberg Brewery in Denmark, whose brewers were responsible for discovering this particular strain.

Adjuncts

Although water, hops, malted barley and yeast are the only things necessary to brew a good beer, additional ingredients are often added by brewers. Some brewers use adjuncts to create different flavors, other brewers use them to cut costs.

These adjuncts could be:

Different grains	Rice, wheat, oats, rye or corn.
Sugars	Honey, maple syrup, dextrose, brown sugar or molasses.
Flavorings	Licorice, spices, fruits.
Chemical additives	Preservatives, antioxidants, foam enhancers, enzymes and stabilizers.

In North America, most of the big brewers make beers with adjuncts. By using corn or rice instead of barley, the breweries can save money. But corn and rice can produce a lighter, less malty beer, something the brewers maintain that the public wants (and who can argue with Budweiser, the world's best-selling beer). In this case, the use of adjuncts is to modify the body or general taste of the beer.

In Germany, the use of anything other than water, hops barley and yeast is prohibited by the German Beer Purity Law. Many microbrewers will add different flavorings to their beer in an effort to produce new and unique products, but these same brewers pride themselves in not adding the chemical additives to their beer.

WHY DO BEERS DIFFER?

In most beers, the only ingredients are water, yeast, hops and malted barley. If these are the only ingredients, then why do beers look, taste and smell so different?

The mass-marketed beers are made to appeal to as broad an audience as possible. To do this, they must be reasonably priced and attempt to be as main-stream as possible. The most popular beers in the world are light bodied, straw colored, mildly hopped and usually served cold. These beers are generally modelled after the Pilsner beers of Bohemia.

But there are a lot of other beers out there on the market that are different from the "popular beers." What makes these beers so different? The differences are due to their production processes more than to their ingredients or additives.

The malt The kilning of the malted barley creates the final color, flavor and aroma of the malt. The color can range from very pale through to almost a black chocolate. As a general principle, the more malt used in the brewing, the more flavorful the beer.

The hops Hops are added to the beer for flavor and aroma and to act as a natural preservative. They give the beer its bitterness when they are added to the brewing early in the boil, and its aroma when they are added later. There is a great variety of hops; some are used for flavor, others for aroma. Brewers may blend these or use them separately to get the effect they want.

The yeast There are basically only two types of yeast: bottom-fermenting and top-fermenting. Bottom-fermenting beers include ales, wheat beers, stouts and porters. All of these beers have fruity notes in their character. Top-fermented products are made at warmer temperatures and they express their full palate when they are served at moderate temperatures. This means that they taste better when they are not served cold!

Top-fermenting beers are fermented at cooler temperatures and then placed in cold storage (this is called lagering). The colder temperatures give the beers a cleaner, softer, mellower taste and, of course, these beers should be served cold.

The water Experts tell us that water is the least important ingredient in beer today. Historically the type of water available to the brewer dictated the type of beer that the brewer could make. But we are told that with modern water treatment facilities the mineral content of any water can be fine-tuned to meet the needs of any style of beer.

However this doesn't explain why the supposedly same beer tastes different in different countries. For example, the Guinness that you get from the St. James Brewery in Dublin tastes much better than the Guinness served elsewhere in the world. Maybe it's the leprechauns, but we suspect that the local water is far more important.

BEER STRENGTHS

Several myths have arisen about the alcoholic strength of beers from different countries. Canadians have always believed that their beers were much stronger than those of their American counterparts. In turn, many Europeans have held the belief that their beers were much more potent than those beers from North America.

These beliefs mostly stem from the confusion over different methods used to measure and express the alcoholic content of beers. In Canada, alcoholic strength is measured by alcohol by volume (ABV), while the Americans use the system of alcohol by weight (ABW).

An alcohol content of 5% by weight means that 5 weight units of alcohol are dissolved into 100 units of a liquid, which in this case is beer. An alcohol content of 5% by volume means that 5 units of alcohol are mixed with 95 units of the liquid (the water) for a total of 100 units. But since alcohol weighs only 79.6 % as much as water, a beer that is 5% alcohol by volume is only 4% by weight (i.e., 79.6% of 5).

The fact is that most Canadian ales and lagers are 5% alcohol by volume and most American beers are 4% alcohol by weight virtually identical. (This gives little credence to the popular Canadian notion of American beer.) The most popular American beers are very light in body and this probably gives the beer drinker the idea that they are light in alcohol as well, which really isn't so. In addition, many states have their own laws about alcoholic content for beer that is sold, for example, in supermarkets, on Sundays, or to minors. As a result, the whole issue about alcoholic content in the United States is quite confusing.

In Britain, the system used to express alcohol in beer is based on the density or original gravity (OG) of the beer. Thus, a beer that is 4% alcohol by weight or 5% alcohol by volume would be described as having an original gravity of 1045 (OG-1045). And just to make things even more puzzling, some countries, like Germany, use the Plato system for expressing alcohol content, and in Belgium the Belge is used.

BEER STRENGTH TABLE

Beer	Alcohol by weight	Alcohol by volume	Original gravity
U.S. regular ales and lagers	3.3-4.2 %	4.6-5.0%	1040-1050
Canadian ales and lagers	3.9-4.1%	4.8-5.0%	1045-1052
U.S. light beers	2.5-3.2%	3.2-3.9%	1030-1036
Canadian light beers	3.3%	4%	1040
British ales and bitters	3.2-3.9%	4-4.8%	1040-1050
European lagers, Pilsners	4%	5%	1048
German wheat beers	4.2-4.5%	5.0-5.6	1048-1058

This table is intended only as a guide. All measurements are only approximations as individual brands may differ.

There are also many strong beers produced throughout the world. For example, barley wine, which is an ale and not a wine, is made by many breweries in Britain. It has an original gravity of 1090–1120, which is over 20% alcohol by volume. Malt liquor, a light-colored beer product produced mostly in the United States, has a high alcohol by volume of around 6 to 8% ABV. In Germany several breweries produce double and triple-bock beers. The alcohol content by volume of these beers is 6% to 12% ABV.

In Canada several high alcohol beers do exist. Molson's Brador is listed as 6% ABV and several of the beers made by Unibroue are well over 5% ABV.

CHAPTER FOUR

Brewing in Canada

As previously mentioned, beer brewing in Canada today is controlled by the two big breweries, Labatt and Molson (affectionately known as the "Big Two").

These companies have many breweries across the country brewing different brands of beer:

- **National brands** available across the country
- **Local brands** usually only available to the local market
- **Contact brands** produced for companies that do not have their own brewing facilities
- **Licensed brands** international brand names brewed for a license fee

Together these two brewing companies produce over 70 different brands of beer in Canada and control over 95% of the Canadian beer market.

LABATT BREWERY

John Labatt began his brewery outside of London, Ontario in 1847. The brewery burned down twice in the late 1800s but persevered into the twentieth century as one of Canada's leaders in the brewing industry.

Some key points in Labatt's history:

1853 John Labatt buys out his partner, Samuel Eccles, and forms the John Labatt Company.

1866 John Labatt Jr. takes over the brewery when his father dies. Under the younger Labatt the brewery expands its market and by 1900 has offices in Toronto and Montreal.

1876 Labatt's brings their new India Pale Ale (IPA), a beer that gains an international reputation and is one of Canada's favorites for years.

1916 Prohibition hits Ontario but Labatt's survives by brewing low alcohol (or temperance beer), and full-strength beer for export.

1945 The company issues 900,000 shares as it becomes a publicly traded firm. A year later it buys the Copeland Brewery in Toronto, its first brewery acquisition.

1950 To mark the 50th anniversary of business in the twentieth century, Labatt's introduces a new light ale, "Annie" (short for anniversary). This beer would later be renamed "50" and become Quebec's favorite.

1951 A new beer, Labatt Pilsner, is launched in Canada. When the beer is introduced in Manitoba, the beer is nicknamed "Blue" for the color of its label and for the uniforms of the Winnipeg Blue Bombers, which Labatt's supports. The nickname sticks and "Blue" is now the number one beer in Canada.

Over the next 20 years Labatt's purchases several out-of-province breweries, including Sheas in Winnipeg, Lucky Lager in British Columbia, Bavarian brewing in Newfoundland, Oland's in Halifax and Saskatoon Breweries. It also builds new breweries in Montreal and Toronto as it embarks on the goal of becoming Canada's national brewer.

In 1995 the John Labatt Brewery was itself acquired by the Belgian conglomerate Interbrew. There are now eight breweries in five regions across the country.

National brands

Labatt Blue, Labatt Blue Light, Labatt 50, Labatt Ice, Labatt Extra Dry, Labatt Genuine Draft, Labatt Select, John Labatt Classic, Lucky Lager, Kokanee, The Wildcat family (low-priced beers), Wildcat, Strong and Light, Old Mick's Red (draft only)

Local brands*

Atlantic Region:	Keith's, Keith's Light, Keith's Dry – brewed in the old Oland's Brewery, Oland Export, Schooner, Blue Star, Jockey Club
Ontario Region:	Select, Crystal, Extra Stock
Quebec Region:	Celtique, 50 Legere, Porter-Quebec
BC Region:	Kootenay, Mountain Ale, True Ale, Black Lager, Pale Ale

Some of these brands are exported to other provinces.

Contract brands

The P.C. line for Loblaws – Strong, Draft, Light, Dry, Red, Czech Gold, Rhinehaus Lager and Kings Cross Ale

Licensed brands

Budweiser, Bud Light, Guinness, Carlsberg, Carlsberg Light, Red, Dark

MOLSON BREWERIES

Molson Breweries is Canada's largest brewery, with seven breweries in seven provinces across Canada. In 1993 a successful alliance with Miller Brewing combined to make Molson the sixth largest brewer in North America.

Notable dates in Molson's history.

1786 John Molson founds the Molson Brewery in Montreal.

1800 First use of bottles for beer.

1844 Beer sold in quart glass bottles.

1903 Molson Export Ale is introduced.

1954 Molson Golden is introduced.

1955 Molson opens brewery in Toronto.

1959 Molson Canadian is introduced.

1971 Molson begins to export its brands to the United States.

1974 Molson takes over the Formosa Brewery plant in Barrie.

1987 The Foster's Group takes over Carling-O'Keefe.

1989 Molson Breweries merges with Foster's Brewing Group.

1993 Molson Breweries forms alliance with Miller Brewing.

Today Molson brews over 60 different brands including Coors, Miller and Foster's for the Canadian market.

National brands

Canadian, Canadian Light, Canadian Ice, Molson Ice, Molson
Black, Molson Dry, Molson Light, Molson Ultra, Molson Ice Ale,
Molson XXX, Molson Signature Cream Ale, Molson Export,
Molson Golden Extra Old Stock, Old Vienna, Carling, Carling
Ice, Carling Light, Carling Strong, Carling Dark, Rickard's Red,
Black Horse, Black Ice, Black Label

Local brands*

Quebec:	Brador, Dow, Grand Nord, Laurentide, Molson Red Jack
Ontario:	Red Dog, Toronto's Own, Stock, Toby
Regina:	Pilsner, Bohemia
St. John's:	Dominion Ale, India
Edmonton,	
Winnipeg,	
Vancouver:	Jack Hammer
Vancouver:	Capilano Pale Ale

Some of these brands are exported to other provinces.

Contract brands

Dave's line of beers: Doppelgold, Ice, Hollander, Light, Strong,
Scotch Ale, Massive Irish, Lager, Belgian Blonde, Cream Ale,
Lemon Lager

Licensed brands

Amstel, Foster's, Foster's Special Bitter, Coors, Coors Light,
Miller, Miller Light, Miller Genuine Draft, Asahi Super Dry,
Milwaukee's Best

MEGA TO MICRO

In Canada it is not hard to keep track of the megabrewers as
there are only two. The "Big Two" are Interbrew, the giant Belgian
corporation that controls Labatt's; and Molson's, which includes the
Carling-O'Keefe division. These two brewers account for about 95%
of the Canadian market. In the United States, Anheuser-Busch, the
brewer of Budweiser, is not only the largest brewer in the USA, but
also in the world. It brews over 90 million barrels of beer annually
or 44% of the USA market. The next four brewers in order of size
in the USA are Miller, Coors, Stroh and Pabst.

Worldwide, some of the other megabrewers include; Heineken (Netherlands), Kirin (Japan), Carlsberg (Denmark), Bass (Great Britain), Guinness (Ireland).

Regional brewers are the smaller, independently owned brewers that produce most of their beer for the local market, although their products are occasionally sold nationally. Examples of regional brewers in Canada are Sleeman and Northern in Ontario; Moosehead in the Maritimes; Pacific Western in British Columbia; and the Big Rock Brewery of Alberta.

The practice of parcelling out the production of beer to a brewery owned by another company is called **contract brewing**. This method of production is used by entrepreneurs who wish to bring out a brand of beer but don't want to put out the cost of building their own brewery. Some examples of contract brewing in Ontario are the Dave's line of beers, brewed by Molson's, and the P.C. line made by Labatt's.

Microbrewers are small breweries that produce fewer than 15,000 barrels a year.

Microbrewers are usually thought of as craft-brewers who produce beer that is more flavorful and distinct than that produced by the big breweries.

Fritz Maytag, heir to the Maytag washing machine fortune, is credited with being one of the founders of the microbrewing industry in North America. In 1965 he bought Anchor Brewing and turned it into an American brewing success story. Using the Anchor Brewing Company as an example, hundreds of microbreweries have sprung up all over North America. At present there are over 110 microbreweries operating in Canada and well over 650 in North America (see Appendix 1).

In brew pubs, beer is brewed on the premises for use in the adjacent bar or restaurant. There are about 90 brew pubs in Canada and over 1300 in the United States. (See brew pubs across Canada in the Appendix 2.) Travellers to the U.S. will have to purchase an American guide book.

REGIONAL BREWERIES

Here is a list of Canada's regional breweries.

BRITISH COLUMBIA

Granville Island Brewing,
1125 Richter St., Kelowna, BC

This brewery, the first modern-day microbrewery in Canada, opened its doors for brewing in 1984. It was located on Granville Island, which is part of Vancouver and attached to it by the Granville Street Bridge. The brewery is still located on Granville Island but its headquarters and bottling plant are located in nearby Kelowna. It is now one of the largest brewers in British Columbia.

Brands: Lord Granville Pale Ale, Island Lager, Gastown Amber Ale, Brockton Black Lager, Cypress Honey Ale, Kitsilano Light, Natural Draft.

Okanagan Spring Brewery, 2801-27A Ave., Vernon, BC

This fairly large brewery was started in an old packing house in Vernon, BC, in the Okanagan Valley in 1985. The company has recently been purchased by Sleeman of Ontario.

Brands: Special Pale Ale, Classic Brown Ale, Honey Blonde Ale, Okanagan Spring Lager, Old English Porter, Old Munich Wheat Beer, Spring Pilsener, St. Patrick's Stout.

Pacific Western Brewing,
641 North Nechako Rd., Prince George, BC

The roots of the Pacific Western Brewery trace back to the Caribou Brewing Company, which was located in Prince George, BC. The brewery lasted through several different ownerships from the 1950s to the late 1980s when it became the Pacific Western.

Brands: Canterbury Dark, Iron Horse, Pacific Dry, Pacific Genuine Draft, Pacific Light, Pacific Pilsener, Pinnacle Amber Ale, Pinnacle Dry Ice, Pinnacle Special Reserve, Traditional Lager, Traditional Light, Traditional Malt, Nature Land Organic Lager.

ALBERTA

Big Rock Brewery

5555 76th Ave. SE, Calgary, AB

The brewery started brewing in 1984. It brews several interesting beers and exports much of its product to the USA. It presently has a large brewery in Calgary and a smaller one in Edmonton.

Brands: Black Amber Ale, Buzzard Breath Ale, Grasshopper Wheat Ale, Magpie Rye Ale, McNally's Extra, Traditional Ale, Warthog Ale, Cock of the Rock, Canvasback Ale.

SASKATCHEWAN

Great Western Brewing

519 2nd Ave. N., Saskatoon, SK

Originally a Carling-O'Keefe brewery, it was closed by Molson's after the amalgamation. In 1991 a group of ex-Molson employees bought it from Molson's and immediately started brewing beer.

Brands: Brewhouse Light, Brewhouse Pilsener, Great Western Gold, Great Western Lager, Great Western Natural Draft, Saskatchewan Beer, Western Premium Light, Christmas Goose.

ONTARIO

Brick Brewing Company

181 King St. S., Waterloo, ON

The little Brick Brewing Company started brewing in 1984. In recent years the company has purchased the Laker brands from Molson's; the Conners brands from the defunct Conners Brewery; and the Algonquin Brewing Company, whose beers are now brewed in Formosa, Ontario.

Brands: Brick: Amber Dry, Hammerhead Red, Henninger Kaiser Pils, Premium Lager, Red Baron Lager, Waterloo Dark.

Conners: Conners Ale, Conners Best Bitter, Conners Dark Ale, Pale Ale, Premium Lager, Special Draft, Stout.

Contract brews: Andrechs Helles Lager, Pacific Real Draft, Movenpick Pilsener.

Algonquin: Algonquin Light, Black and Tan, Country Lager, Formosa Draft, Formosa Light, Honey Brown Lager, Royal

Amber Lager, Bavarian Bock, Special Reserve Dark Ale.

Lakeport Brewing

201 Burlington St. E., Hamilton, ON

The Lakeport Brewery was launched in 1992 in the building that once housed the Amstel brewing operations. It now brews many different brands including their own labels, contract brands and licensed products.

Brands: Lakeport Dry, Lakeport Light, Lakeport Pilsener, Lakeport Strong, Bartenders Choice Lager, Lone Star Lager, Lone Star Light, Masters Choice Pilsener, Masters Choice Strong, Masters Choice, Tipperary Dark Irish Lager, McGinty's Irish, Mont Tremblant Amber, Mont Tremblant Pilsener, Norois, Norois Dry, Ontario 7.3, Pabst Blue Ribbon, Ranier Lager, Steel City Lager.

Northern Breweries

503 Bay St., Sault Ste. Marie, ON

The history of Northern Breweries dates back to the early 1900s. By 1960 Doran's had acquired five breweries in the north (Sudbury, Sault Ste. Marie, Kakabeka Falls, Port Arthur and Timmins) to form Doran's Northern Breweries. Canadian Breweries took the operation over in 1971 and then sold it to the employees in 1977.

Brands: 55 Lager, Edelbrau Lager, Northern Ale, Northern Extra Light Lager, Superior Lager, Thunder Lager.

Sleeman Brewing and Malting Company

551 Clair Rd. W., Guelph, ON

The Sleeman Malting and Brewing Company can trace its roots back to John Sleeman's great-great-grandfather who started brewing beer in Canada in 1834. The modern-day Sleeman's opened its doors in Guelph in 1988. The company now owns the Okanagan Spring and Shaftbury breweries in British Columbia, the Seigneuriale in Quebec and, most recently, the Upper Canada Brewery in Toronto. The Upper Canada brands are now brewed at the Sleeman Brewery in Guelph.

Brands: Sleeman Cream Ale, Silver Creek Lager, Sleeman Honey Brown Lager, Sleeman Light, Sleeman Dark, Sleeman Steam Ale, Upper Canada Dark Ale, Upper Canada Lager, Upper

Canada Light, Upper Canada Maple Brown Ale, Natural Point 9, Rebellion Ale, Rebellion Lager, Upper Wheat.

QUEBEC

Unibroue

80 Des Carrieres, Chambly, PQ

In 1991 Unibroue started brewing Belgian-style beers in the defunct Massawippi Brewing Company in Lennoxville. The beers brewed offer a different variety of tastes not normally found in Canada, including several Belgian-style beers.

Brands: Maudite, La Fin Du Monde, Eau Benite, Blanche de Chambly, Raftman, La Gaillarde, Quelque Chose, Trois Pistoles, La Fleurdelysse Clarisse.

NEW BRUNSWICK

Moosehead

89 Main St., Saint John, NB

Because of antiquated laws in many provinces it was almost impossible for Moosehead to sell beer to the rest of the country for many years. As a result Moosehead was one of the more popular imports in the United States and in the United Kingdom, but unavailable to most Canadians. Fortunately the situation has changed and Moosehead is now available across the country.

The brewery is owned and operated by the Oland family who trace their roots in brewing as far back as 1867 in Nova Scotia. The family business split in the 1920s and one branch of the family moved to New Brunswick to open what would later become Moosehead Breweries.

Brands: Moosehead Beer, Moosehead Canadian Lager, Moosehead Canadian Ice, Moosehead Canadian Light, Moosehead Dry Ice, Moosehead Mariner Ale, Moosehead Mariner Beer, Moosehead Premium Dry, Moosehead Pale Ale, Alpine, Alpine Genuine Cold Filtered Alpine Light, Clancy's Amber Ale, Ten Penny Old Stock Ale.

Ten Canadian beers you should try

These are not necessarily the top 10 beers in Canada but a sampling of the different beers available.

- **Creemore Springs Premium Lager**
  Creemore Springs Brewery; a smooth hoppy well-balanced lager.
- **Wellington County Ale**
  Wellington County Brewery, Guelph; usually hand-pulled draft only; cask-conditioned.
- **Eisbock**
  Niagara Falls Brewing Company; North America's first ice beer 8% ABV – limited edition; bottled like champagne.
- **Big Rock Warthog Ale**
  A mild nutty-flavored beer; similar to a Northern English brown ale.
- **St. Ambroise Oatmeal Stout**
  Brasserie McAuslan, Montreal; a thick black chocolatey stout.
- **Old Peculiar Strong Ale**
  Granite Breweries, Halifax and Toronto; originally only available on draft, it is now contract brewed and bottled by the Hart Brewing Company.
- **La Maudite**
  Unibroue, Chambly, Quebec; a Belgian-styled strong ale at 8% ABV; this brewery produces many fine Belgian beer styles.
- **Amsterdam Nut Brown Ale**
  Amsterdam Brewing Company, Toronto; a smooth example of what a brown ale should be.
- **Muskoka Cream Ale**
  Lakes of Muskoka Cottage Brewery, Bracebridge; a quality smooth ale.
- **Dave's Scotch Ale**
  Marketed by Dave's but brewed by Molson's; you can't beat the price and this is a pretty good Scottish-style ale.

CHAPTER FIVE

Brewing in the United States

"Beer is proof that God loves us and wants us to be happy."
– Benjamin Franklin (former brewer)

Contrary to popular opinion, the beers made in the United States are not low in alcoholic content. They are the same as beers made in the rest of the world (4 to 5% ABV). The United States does, however, lead the world in the production of light-bodied, light-tasting, light-colored beers. These beers are modelled after the Pilsner style originated in Bohemia. Many of these American beers are so light and fizzy that many Canadians consider them to be "near beers" and treat them with scorn. But this is an unfair and incorrect judgement.

Alcoholic Content of American Beer Styles

Style	Original Gravity (OG)	Alcohol by Volume (ABV)
Light beer (lager)	1.020-1.040	3.5-4.5
Standard lager	1.040-1.047	3.8-4.8
Premium lager	1.046-1.050	4.4-5.0
Ice beer	1.046-1.050	4.4-5.0
Dry beer	1.040-1.050	3.8-5.0
Amber ale	1.040-1.055	4.5-5.5
Malt liquor	1.044-1.052	4.8-5.8

At last count there were 42 large breweries, 535 microbreweries and around 1300 brew pubs making beer in the United States. It is also interesting to note that five out of the top 10 beers sold in the country are light beers.

Here are the top 10 brewers in the United States.

ANHEUSER-BUSCH – St. Louis, Missouri.

The largest brewer in the U.S. and in the entire world.

In 1860 Eberhard Anheuser purchased a small brewery in St. Louis called the Bavarian Brewery. Four years later Adolphus Busch, Anheuser's son-in-law, began working as a salesman for the brewery. Eventually Adolphus became a partner and the driving force in the business.

Busch wanted to brew a beer that would be popular with everyone. In the late 1800s the most popular beers brewed in the United States were those modelled after the beers from central Europe. Busch decided to fashion the brewery's new beer after the Pilsner beers found in Bohemia. In 1876 Adolphus decided to call their new beer Budweiser, named after "Budweiss" made in Bohemia. Today Budweiser is the largest-selling single brand of beer in the United States and in the world.

Budweiser became so successful not necessarily because of its flavor or quality, but because Busch came up with the idea of marketing the beer nationwide, providing distribution through the use of refrigerated railway cars.

Brands:

Budweiser family

Budweiser, called "The King of Beers" because the original beer, Budweiss, was once the brewery of the royal court of Bohemia. Today one out of every four beers consumed in the United States is a Budweiser.

Bud Light: introduced in 1982, Bud Light became the number one light beer in the United States in 1995. It is now the number two selling beer in the country.

Bud Ice, Bud Ice Light.

Michelob family

Michelob: Originally introduced in 1896 as a draft beer, it is billed as Anheuser-Busch's premium beer. Michelob Light, Michelob Dry, Michelob Dark.

Other brands:

Busch, Busch Light, Busch Ice, Natural, Natural Light, Natural

Ice Winter Brew Spiced Ale, O'Doul's (non-alcoholic).

Specialty Brews:

Red Wolf, Ziegen Bock, Pacific Ridge Pale Ale, Black and Tan Porter, Honey Lager, Hefeweizen, Amber Bock, Pale Ale, Porter.

MILLER BREWING COMPANY – Milwaukee, Wisconsin.

The Miller Brewing Company is the second largest brewery in the United States with six breweries located across the country. In 1850 members of the Best family founded the Plank Road Brewery in Milwaukee (this same family also founded the Pabst Brewery). Five years later this brewery was sold to a young German brewer named Frederick Miller. And shortly thereafter it was renamed the Frederick Miller Brewing Company. It remained in the Miller family until 1970 when it was purchased by the Philip Morris Company.

In the early 1970s Miller brought out a new beer that they called "Miller Lite". This beer became so popular that it eventually became the second best-selling beer (behind Budweiser) in the United States. The huge sales of these beers ushered in a new style of beer, light beer, to the forefront of American beer consumption. More recently, Miller Lite has fallen to number three, behind Bud Light.

In the 1990s Miller joined forces with Molson, the Canadian brewing giant, agreeing to distribute their products across the USA. In 1999 Miller expanded again, purchasing the Henry Weinhard's and Mickey's brands from Stroh's. It will probably come as a surprise that Miller either produces or distributes over 57 brands of beer.

Brands:

Miller family

Miller Beer, Miller Lite, Lite Ice, Genuine Draft, Genuine Draft Light, High Life, High Life Ice, High Life Light.

Icehouse

Milwaukee's Best, Milwaukee's Best Light Red Dog, Milwaukee's Best Ice, Meister Brau, Meister Brau Light, Magnum, Southpaw Light, Sharp's, Leinenkugel Family (Craft Brews Family), Auburn Ale, Autumn Gold, Berry Weiss, Doppelbock, Genuine Bock, Hefeweizen, Honey Weiss, Maple Brown Lager, Northwoods Lager, Red Lager Original, Winter Lager, Shipyard Export Ale,

Shipyard Goat Island Light Ale, Shipyard Pale Ale, Shipyard Longfellow Winter Ale, Shipyard Brown Ale, Shipyard Blue Fin Stout, Old Thumper Extra Special Ale, Mystic Seaport Pale Ale.

COORS BREWING COMPANY—Golden, Colorado

The Coors Brewing Company operates the largest single-site brewery in the world and is now the third largest brewer in the U.S. It is capable of producing over 20 million barrels of beer per year. Coors remains a family-owned brewery and was founded in 1873, three years before Colorado became the 38th state. Jacob Scheuler and Adolph Coors opened "The Golden Brewery" and soon were shipping their beer to thirsty miners in the foothills of the Rockies. Several years later Coors bought out Scheuler's share of the company and renamed it the Adolph Coors Golden Brewery.

In 1959 Coors introduced the country's first all-aluminum beer can, but because of its limited distribution, Coors remained a primarily regional company.

In the 1970s, however, Coors built up their distribution system and began shipping its beer all over the country. It became very successful as the beer "Brewed with Pure Rocky Mountain Spring Water."

The original Coors, first brewed in 1874, was called "Coors Banquet" and was the flagship brew for the company for many years. Recently, though, Coors Light (the "Silver Bullet"), introduced in 1978, became their number one selling beer and the number four brand in the United States. Up until 1970 the only beer that Coors brewed was the original Coors. Since then the brewery has greatly expanded its range of beers and includes a craft-brewing subsidiary.

Brands:
Coors family
Original Coors, Coors Light, Coors Extra Gold, Coors Arctic Ice, Coors Arctic Ice Light, Coors Cutter.
Irish family
George Killians – Irish Red Lager, Wilde Honey Ale, Irish Brown Ale.
Blue Moon Brewing (Coors' craft-brewing division)
Blue Moon Belgian White Ale, Honey Blonde Ale, Nut Brown Ale, Raspberry Cream Ale, Harvest Pumpkin Ale.

Keystone Family (Coors' popular-priced beers)

Keystone, Light, Dry, Ice Amber.

The Stroh Brewing Company—Detroit, Michigan.

Until recently Stroh's was the fourth largest brewery in the United States. It was founded in 1850 in Detroit by Bernard Strohand, originally known as the Lion Brewery. The name was changed to the Stroh Brewing company in the early 1900s.

Stroh began brewing a beer that was lighter than the traditional ales of the day, calling the brew his "Bohemian beer." To distinguish his brand he adopted the ancient crest of Bohemia, a gold lion on a red background. Stroh's soon became one of the most popular beers in America often advertised as America's "fire-brewed beer." This was a reference to their technique of using direct flames to heat their brewing kettles.

In the early 1980s Stroh's acquired both the Schaefer and Schlitz Breweries and became the third largest brewery in the United States. In 1996 Stroh's purchased the Heileman Brewing Company. In 1999 Stroh's sold off its brands to Miller Brewing and Pabst Brewing. Miller agreed to buy Stroh's Henry Weinhard's and Mickey's brands, while Pabst bought the rest of the Stroh's brands, including Stroh's, Old Milwaukee and Schlitz.

Pabst Brewing Company—Milwaukee, Wisconsin.

Now the fourth largest brewing company in the United States, Pabst can trace its brewing history back to 1840 when Jacob Best relocated his brewery from Germany to Milwaukee. He called his new brewery the Empire Brewery, the first company to brew beer in Milwaukee.

In 1850 two of his sons left the business and began the Plank Road Brewery (now the Miller Brewing Company). In 1862 Frederick Pabst, a steamer captain, married into the Best family and soon joined the company. Pabst and partner bought the company in 1865 and it was eventually renamed the Pabst Brewing Company.

By 1893 Pabst was recognized as "America's Best Lager Beer" at the World Columbian Exposition and given the first-place blue ribbon. From then on it was known as "Pabst Blue Ribbon Beer." It soon became one of the most popular beers in America.

Over the years Pabst has taken several breweries including Ballantine, Faltsaff, Hamm's, General and, most recently, Pearl and Stroh's.

Brands
Pabst family
Pabst Blue Ribbon, Pabst Genuine Draft, Hamm's Olde English 800, Olympia Stag Weidemann.

New brands
Stroh's, Old Milwaukee, Schlitz.

Genesee Brewing Company—Rochester, New York
The Genesee Brewing Company is the largest independent regional brewery and the fifth largest operation in the United States. It was founded in 1878 but disappeared when Prohibition hit the U.S. The company was reorganized by Louis Wehle, a former brewmaster, in 1933.

Genesee has only one massive brewery, hence their slogan, "One Brewery, One Great Taste." It is remarkable to be on the list as the fifth largest brewer since it only distributes to 26 states and two Canadian provinces. Their flagship brand, Genesee Cream Ale, is known as "Genny" throughout upper New York State.

Brands:
Genesee family
Genesee Cream Ale, Genny Light, Genny Ice, Genesee 12 Horse Ale, Genny Bock, Genny Red.

Koch's Golden Anniversary Beers, Light, Ice, J.W. Dundee's Honey Brown Lager, Michael Shea's Irish Amber, Black and Tan, Blonde Lager.

Boston Beer Company—Boston, Massachusetts.
The Boston Beer Company, now the sixth largest in the United States, was founded by sixth-generation brewer Jim Koch, in 1984. Many of the recipes for the Boston were passed down from his predecessors.

The brewery leads the country in the specialty beer market, producing many unique beers, including their flagship beers, Samuel Adams Boston Lager and Samuel Adams Boston Ale. It is the preeminent contract-brewing firm as almost all of its brews are produced by contract by various companies throughout the country.

Brands:
Sam Adams Boston family
Boston Lager, Boston Ale, Scotch Ale, White Ale, Golden Pilsner, Triple Bock, Lightship, Honey Porter, Cream Stout, Cherry Wheat.
Seasonal Brews
Octoberfest, Cranberry Lambic, Winter Lager, Double Bock, Spring Ale, Summer Ale.

McKenzie River Partners—San Francisco, California.
This San Francisco brewery is one of the top ten brewers in America. It is the number one contract brewer in the country and brews only a few of its own beers. One is the infamous St. Ides Malt Liquor.

St. Ides Malt Liquor

Malt liquor is described as one of the choice beverages for "gansta" rappers. In the early 1990s McKenzie River was criticized for using rap stars like the Geto Boys and Ice Cube to promote its high-alcohol malt liquor. In television commercials the groups recounted how the drink was good for them. A line from an Ice Cube ad said that the malt liquor would "get your girl in the mood quicker and get your Jimmy thicker."

Pearl Brewing Company—San Antonio, Texas.
The Pearl Brewing Company of San Antonio, Texas, was founded in 1881. It was the ninth largest brewer in the United States until it was taken over by the Pabst Brewery.

Brands:
Pearl Beer, Pearl Light, Jax, Falstaff, 900 Malt Liquor.

Latrobe—Latrobe Pennsylvania.

The United States' tenth largest brewery was founded in Latrobe, Pennsylvania in 1893. It is one of the few regional breweries to survive. The main product brewed by Latrobe is their Rolling Rock beer, which is bottled in the familiar green bottle with the retro white ceramic label. It also brews a very fine Bavarian Black Beer.

Latrobe was bought by Labatt's in 1987.

Anchor Brewing Company—San Francisco, California.

This brewery was originally founded in San Francisco in 1896. It was on the verge of collapse in 1965 when Fritz Maytag, heir to the Maytag washing machine fortune, bought a stake in it. When he took over the company Maytag reintroduced the old recipes and turned Anchor into the first craft brewery since before Prohibition.

Anchor Steam Beer, the brewery's flagship beer, was based on the legendary "steam beers" produced in San Francisco during the gold rush days. Today it produces one of the most prized premium craft beers in the world.

The success of the Anchor Brewing Company has been an inspiration for all the microbreweries to follow.

Brands:

Anchor Steam Beer, Anchor Porter, Liberty Ale.

D.G. Yuengling & Son Brewing Company—Pottsville, Pennsylvania.

Distinguished as being the oldest continuously operated brewery in the United States, D.G. Yuengling & Son was founded in 1829 and is still a family-owned business. The brewery certainly suffered some lean times in the 1960s and 1970s, but in recent days with the increased interest in microbrewed beers, D.G. Yuengling is again a prosperous operation.

Brands:

Lord Chesterfield Ale, Yuengling Premium, Yuengling Porter, Bavarian Premium Beer, Old German Beer.

Pittsburg Brewing Company—Pittsburg, Pennsylvania.

The Pittsburgh Brewing Company was formed in 1899 when 16 breweries in the Pittsburgh area joined together. Initially it was bought out by Heileman's and is now a part of the Pabst brewing family.

Today Pittsburg Brewing is a very large contract brewer, producing such beers as Sam Adams Lager for the Boston Beer Company. It also brews several beers of its own.

Brands:

Iron City Beer, Old German Beer.

Celis Brewing Company—Austin, Texas.

This brewery was founded in1991 by Pierre Celis who worked at the Hoegaarden Brewery in Belgium. It is unique in the United states because it brews Belgium-styled beers. In 1995 the brewery formed an alliance with Miller brewing who now markets and distributes the beers.

Brands:

Celis Dubbel Ale, Golden, Grand Cru, Pale Ale, Pale Bock, Raspberry, White.

CHAPTER SIX

Brewing in Europe

"Blessing of your heart, you brew good ale."
- William Shakespeare

BRITAIN

Britain (England, Northern Ireland, Scotland and Wales) ranks sixth in the world in the production of beer, but only ninth in beer consumption per capita.

There are over 200 breweries and over 70,000 pubs in Britain. There used to be six mega British breweries: Allied Lyons, Bass Charrington, Courage, Scottish and Newcastle, Watney and Whitbread. In 1966 Bass purchased the Allied group to become the largest brewing company in Britain and, more recently, Scottish and Newcastle took over Courage. As a result Bass now controls 35% of the beer market in Britain while Scottish Courage controls 31%.

Most beer consumed in Britain is consumed in the pub. The traditional drink in Britain is ale, unlike the rest of the world where lager is king. (Belgium is the only other country where the sales of ale exceed those of lager.)

It is a common misconception that British beer is served warm. In truth, British ales should be served at cellar temperature, which is 13°C. Since ales are top-fermented at warmer temperatures, they taste best when they are served at a warmer temperature, while lagers are best consumed cold. In countries outside of Britain, British ales are often served too cold, preventing the beer drinker from appreciating their proper taste. Quite often the comment is that the "beer doesn't travel well" and therefore doesn't taste like it does back home. In fact, the beer has just been served at the wrong temperature or like many imported draft beers, it has been pasteurized, a process that can drastically affect the taste.

British ales can be classified into several categories:

- **Bitter** In reality, these beers aren't all that bitter. The name comes from the days when most breweries produced two ales, a mild and a bitter. The mild was a sweeter-tasting beer and than the bitter. Bitter is a dry, highly hopped beer that accounts for more than 80% of draft beer sold in Britain. Bitter can be served as ordinary bitter and as "best" bitter. Ordinary bitter has a lower gravity or alcoholic content (usually about 4% ABV). Best bitter has a higher alcoholic content of 5% or more. There are hundreds of tastes in bitter ales. Some bitters can be malty, fruity, dry-hopped, soft, biting, sweet, light or heavy.

- **Pale ale** The actual color of pale ale isn't really pale but usually a reddish or a copper brown. Before modern development, beers were either dark or cloudy, consequently this style of beer became known as "pale ale." The term India Pale Ale (IPA) is often used interchangeably with pale ale. In the 1800s British brewers wanted to send beer to the troops stationed in India. To survive the long sea voyage the ale was brewed to a high alcohol content and heavily hopped to protect it from infection. Many brewers in Britain still use the term for their pale ale. This style was especially associated with the town of Burton-on-Trent.

- **Porter** This dark robust beer was introduced in London in the early 1700s. It is usually higher in alcoholic content (5 to 6% ABV) than other beers. The name "porter" was coined because of its popularity with that group of workers. In the early 1800s porter was the most popular beer style in England. The style spread to Ireland, where it was brewed by Guinness. Eventually the Irish porter was made much stronger and called stout. While it is not an extremely popular beer today, a few breweries have revived the style and many microbreweries are actively producing porter all over the world.

The British Pub

There is nothing more unique than the British pub.

The word "pub" comes from public house, a place where people could go to rest and receive good hospitality. The landlord who runs the pub may be correctly called the "publican."

In Britain almost everyone goes to the pub, whether they drink beer or not. Most have their "local" where they feel comfortable and relax with friends or family.

Pubs date back to medieval times when the abbeys and priories offered drink, food and lodging to those travelling through their towns. The local people would come to meeting places to hear news from other parts of the country. In the early days, the church not only sold the beer but made it as well, running and controlling these houses. In many small towns the church and pub stand side by side and, in some cases, you can see where they were once attached to each other.

Much of Britain's history can be told via the pub since it has always been such an integral part of the culture. Many pubs can tell a story, often exhibited by their names: The Quiet Woman, The Bucket of Blood, The Duke Without a Head, The Busby Stoop, The Trip to Jerusalem, to mention a few.

There are three types of British pubs today:

Tied houses

These are pubs that are owned by the breweries. Here the brewery can market its own brands of beer. The big megabreweries own thousands of their own pubs.

Free houses

These are pubs owned by individuals. The owners can serve their own choice of beers. They often bring in "guest" beers to augment their regular brands.

Pub chains

These are a series of pubs all owned by the same individual or company, or franchised out by the company. Many of these are brew pubs. Examples would be the Firkin pubs in London and The Little Pub Company in the West Midlands.

- **Mild** This is a dark brown ale that is sweet and low in alcoholic content (3 to 3.5% ABV). Mild beer is described as being low in hops and having malty, almost fruity undertones. Mild was originally brewed as a beverage to refresh manual workers' thirst because hoppy brews were often drying in the throat. Later it became a brew for miners and mill workers, and at one time all of the breweries made a mild. It is still a popular draft beer in the English Midlands.
- **Brown ale** There are two types of brown ale produced in Britain. In the southern part of England the beer is very dark, sweet and fairly low in alcohol content. The best example of a southern brown ale is Mann's Brown Ale. The other brown ale, which is more popular in the north, is amber brown, less sweet and has a higher alcohol content. One of these is Samuel Smith's Nut Brown Ale, a rich nutty-tasting beer. Another is probably the best-known brown ale in the world, Newcastle Brown Ale. This beer is brewed in the city of Newcastle, England, and purists insist it is best out of the bottle, rather than a can.
- **Stout** Stout has several different styles. It is made with deeper-roasted malt than other beers and has a coffee-like taste. English stout is a sweet stout and was once referred to as "milk stout," recommended for nursing mothers. The best example of English stout is Mackeson's Stout. Oatmeal stout is a variation of sweet stout and a popular brand of this is Samuel Smith's Oatmeal Stout.
- **Barley wine** Barley wine is not a wine but rather an ale that tastes as strong as wine. It comes in small bottles and is normally served in a small wine glass or brandy snifter. It is usually strong in flavor, sometimes fruity or caramelly and quite high in alcohol content (7 to 15% ABV). Like other beers, barley wines come in both dark or pale styles.

Some of the important breweries in England

Brewery	Location	Beers
Bass Brewers Founded 1777	Burton-on-Trent	Bass Ale, Worthington White Shield
Ind Cooper Founded 1845	Burton-on-Trent	Double Diamond, Burton Ale, Ansell's Mild
Samuel Smith Old Brewery Founded 1758	Tadcaster, North Yorkshire	Old Brewery Pale Ale, Nut Brown Ale, Taddy Porter Oatmeal Stout, Imperial Stout
John Smith's Brewery Founded 1883	Tadcaster, North Yorkshire	John Smith's Bitter, John Smith's Magnet, Webster's Yorkshire Bitter
Theakston's Brewery Founded 1827	Masham, North Yorkshire	Old Peculiar (no, it's not misspelled), Best Bitter, Mild, XB
Young and Co. Founded 1675	London	Ordinary Bitter, Special Bitter, Ram Rod, Special London Ale, Old Nick Barleywine
Fuller, Smith and Turner Founded 1845	London	Chiwick Bitter, London Pride Bitter, ESB Premium Bitter
Eldridge, Pope & Co. Founded 1837	Dorchester	Thomas Hardy's Ale (Old Dorset Ale), Royal Oak Pale Ale, Thomas Hardy Country Bitter, Dorchester Bitter

| **Wadworth & Co.** | Devizes, Wiltshire | 6X, Original IPA |

| **Tetley & Son** Founded 1822 | Leeds, West Yorkshire | Tetley Bitter, Tetley Mild |

| **Boddington's** Founded 1778 | Manchester | Boddington Cream, Manchester Gold Bitter |

| **Shepherd Neame** Founded 1698 | Faversham, Kent | Bishop's Finger, Spitfire Porter, Best Bitter |

Courage
Founded 1787
A division of Scottish Courage with four breweries in England:

| **Newcastle, Tyne Brewery** | Newcastle-upon-Tyne | Newcastle Brown Ale, Newcastle Exhibition |

| **Bristol Brewery** | Bristol, Avon | Courage Best Bitter, Courage Directors Bitter |

| **Royal Brewery** | Manchester | Licensed brand lagers: Foster's, Molson, Coors, |

| **Berkshire Brewery** | Reading, Berkshire | Licensed brand lagers: Miller, Hofmeister, Foster's, Kronenbourg |

| **Marston, Thompson & Evershed** Founded 1834 | Burton-on-Trent | Pedigree Pale Ale, Marston's Bitter, Owd Roger Old Ale, Oyster Stout |

| **Greene King** Founded 1789 | Bury St. Edmonds | Abbot Ale, Strong Suffolk |

SCOTLAND

The basic beer brewed in Scotland is called Scottish ale, usually a pale ale that is well malted. In the early 1900s, the malts were dried with peat moss, the same way that Scotch whisky malt is dried. This gave the Scottish ales a heavy, smoky taste, not unlike the single malts. Modern-day Scottish ales have a sweeter maltiness and little of the original "scotch whisky" taste.

Scottish ales are made with dark roasted malts and are not as hoppy as English ales. There are three types of Scottish ales:

- **Scottish light ale** is a counterpart to the English mild. It is usually light in alcohol content and dark in color. A customer might ask for a "light" or "sixty shilling."
- **Scottish heavy ale** compares to the regular bitter served in England. It is normally a little paler than the light ale (a fact that confuses tourists all the time). Heavy has a higher alcohol content. As well as being called a "heavy," it is also called "seventy shilling."
- **Scottish export ale** is like a premium bitter in that it is much hoppier than the other two beers. It will often be referred to as "eighty shilling."

In addition one may encounter a "wee heavy," which is similar to a barley wine and served in small bottles called "nips."

The nostalgic shilling system

In Scotland and in many parts of England some beers are called 60 (sixty shilling), 70 (seventy shilling) and 80 (eighty shilling). This refers to the old money used in Great Britain and it is said that it was the past tax rate on a cask of beer. Beers of a lower alcohol content were taxed at lower rate than beers that were higher on alcohol content.

Some of the major breweries in Scotland

Brewery	Location	Beers
Caledonian Brewing Co. Founded 1869	Edinburgh	Scottish Ales 60, 70, 80, Deudars IPA, Murray's Heavy, Edinburgh Strong Ale
Broughton Brewery Founded 1980	Biggar	Greenmantle, Merlins Old Jock, Special Bitter, Scottish Oatmeal Stout
Maclay & Co. Founded 1830	Alloa	Scottish Ales 60, 70, 80, Wallace IPA
McEwan's Old Fountain Brewery Founded 1836	Edinburgh	McEwan's Scotch Ale, Youngers
Traquair House	Peebleshire	Traquair House Ale Bear Ale, Jacobite

The Traquair Manor House dates back to the twelfth century. While renovating in 1965, the owners discovered an old brewery. This part of the house was restored and a new brewery was opened in 1965, specializing in brewing Scottish ale from old recipes.

Belhaven Brewing Founded in 1719 – now Scotland's oldest brewery	Dunbar	Sandy Hunters Ale St. Andrews Ale

WALES

The Welsh beers are very similar in style and taste to their English counterparts.

Here are a few of the more important breweries in Wales.

Brewery	Location	Beers
Brain & Co. Founded 1882	Cardiff	Brain's Bitter, Brain's Dark, Brain's SA (known as "Skull attack" by the Locals), Brain's Smooth
Crown Buckley Founded 1767	Llannelli	Buckley's Best Bitter, Buckley's Dark Mild, Crown Pale Ale, Reverend James, Original Ale
Felinfoel Brewing Founded 1878	Llannelli	Double Dragon Ale (also called Welsh Ale), Dragon Dark, Dragon Bitter

IRELAND

Guinness

Ireland is the place to drink stout, dry stout that is. Stout evolved from the brewing of porter by Arthur Guinness. In 1759 he purchased an old rundown brewery in Dublin on St. James Gate. Guinness decided to try his hand at brewing to compete with the imports from England. His new beer was made with roasted barley, which gave the beer a very dark, almost black color. It was also rich in flavor and soon became the most popular beer in Dublin. This beer was originally called Guinness Extra Stout Porter because it was a stronger, more full-bodied beer. Eventually the "porter" was dropped and the rest is history.

By 1825 Guinness was available abroad and by 1838 it was the largest brewery in Ireland. By 1914, the Guinness brewery on St. James Gate was the largest brewery in the world. Now no longer the largest single brewery, it is brewed under license in 35 countries in the world and it is sold in over 150 counties around the world, making it the greatest international beer.

Waiting for that perfect pint of Guinness

Guinness is best served slightly cooler (5° to 8°C) than most other ales. It does take time to pour that pint in your favorite pub. That's because the brewing company has given specific instructions as to how their beer should be served. Special taps are provided to properly mix the 75% nitrogen and 25% carbon dioxide used to give the brew its wonderful creamy brown head, a head that should last to the bottom of the glass.

- When the beer is poured, you should be able to put your initials in the head of foam and see it last to the bottom of the glass. The pouring takes time as the bartender is supposed to hold the glass tilted at 45° until it is three-quarters full. He should then allow the head to settle before filling the glass up to the top.
- Draft Guinness in Canada is brewed by Molson's. This beer is about 5% ABV, which is a little higher than the "liquid gold" produced in Ireland, but Guinness standards state that all overseas brews must contain the flavored extract that is brewed at St. James Gate in Dublin.
- The Guinness "draft flow" canned beer has a widget that that releases a small amount of nitrogen through the beer producing the famous Guinness head just like the real draft. This beer is produced Ireland and is 4.1% ABV.

Every day more than 10 million pints of Guinness are consumed. Draft Guinness in Ireland is unpasteurized because of the large keg turnover. Perhaps that is why a pint of Guinness tastes better in Ireland than anywhere else.

It is common practice to mix Guinness with other beverages. One of the most popular mixed drinks is called Black Velvet, a mixture of Guinness and champagne. Local legend alleges that this drink was first served in the observance of the death of Prince Albert, Queen Victoria's husband. Folklore says that the champagne represented the nobility while the Guinness stood for the commoners who adored Albert.

True Guinness drinkers insist that it should take exactly seven sips to down a standard pint of their beer and that each of these sips should leave a ring of foam down the side of the glass. You might have to seek out an Irish man to learn how to perfect this technique.

Breweries in Ireland

Brewery	Location	Beers
Arthur Guinness & Sons Founded 1759	Dublin	Draught Guinness, Guinness Extra Stout
Arthur Guinness	Dundalk	Harp Lager
Beamish & Crawford Founded 1792	Cork	Beamish Stout, Beamish Red Irish Ale
Murphy Brewery Founded 1854	Cork	Murphy's Irish Stout, Irish Red Ale
Smithwick & Sons Founded 1710 Ireland's oldest brewery	Kilkenny	Smithwick's Ale, Kilkenny Irish Ale

GERMANY

With over 1200 breweries and one of the greatest beer consumptions per capita in the world, Germany has to be considered one of the predominant brewing nations. Germans consume about 137 litres per person per year. There is, however, a south to north differential: drinkers in the southern state of Bavaria drink far more beer than their countrymen to the north. It is estimated that Bavarians consume well over 200 litres a person per year.

It often assumed that all German beers are lagers, but this is not true. In fact the term "lager" is not normally used as Germans have several varieties of this type of beer.

Germans for the most part enjoy their beer outside of the home, in beer gardens or beer halls. In Bavaria almost every town or village has its own brewery. As a result Germans have a great choice in their beer consumption – far more than Canadians.

Styles of German Beer

- **Alt** (Altbier) In German, *alt* is the word for "old" but here the term does not refer to the beer being old or aged for a long time. Instead it means that the beer is brewed according to an old tradition. Alt is a beer that has long been associated with the city of Duesseldorf. It is a hybrid beer in that is top-fermented like an ale, then cold-aged like a lager. Depending on the recipe, alt may have a highly hopped, bitter taste or a malty-sweet taste. It is normally dark with a medium body.

- **Bock** It's hard to believe that bock beer is bottom-fermented like lager. While bock is normally very dark and malty-sweet, sometimes even with a chocolatey taste, it is hopped to balance out the sweetness. The name originates from the town of Einbeck in northern Germany. The beer produced became known as "beck," which with a Bavarian accent sounded like "bock." The German translation for bock is "goat" and that is why so many brands of bock beer have a goat as their symbol.

  Contrary to legend, bock is not produced once a year when the breweries clean out their tanks and bottle the stuff at the bottom as bock! At one time it was brewed in the late fall, aged over the winter and served in the spring. Nowadays it is still seasonal but different breweries decide on which season they will brew it. Bock is higher in alcohol content than most beers. There is also a light-colored bock called Helles Bock or Maibock.

- **Doppelbock** (double bock) is a stronger version of bock. It was originally brewed by the monks of St. Francis Paula. This beer, which is very high in alcohol, was given to the monks at Lent. They called this brew "liquid bread" and were probably very happy monks indeed! The St. Pauline brewery, now standing on the site of the monastery, named their doppelbock Salvator in homage to the saviour. This beer is usually brought out at Easter.

- **Eisbock** is the strongest of the bock beers. Regular doppelbock is brewed and then the beer temperature is lowered to 0°C. Although the water freezes, the alcohol does not. Ice is then removed leaving behind a beer with a very high alcohol content. It is quite full-bodied, sweet and lightly hopped.

Hofbrauhaus

Without a doubt this is the most famous beer drinking establishment in the world. Located in Munich, Hofbrauhaus is over 400 years old. It is, in fact, a brewery, a beer hall and a beer garden, all in one. It can accommodate over 4500 people at one time and is often very noisy and busy. Haufbrauhaus means "royal court brewing," referring to the times when the local royalty controlled the beer-making industry. Now owned by the state of Bavaria, it attracts large numbers of tourists, especially during Oktoberfest. Its famous HB steins can be found all over the world.

- **Dortmunder** Also called Export, this beer is from the city of Dortmund. This city makes more beer than any other in Germany. There are over 30 different brands produced with the name Dortmund on them. Export is a bottom-fermented beer similar to Pilsner, but not as hoppy. It has a strong malty-sweet taste.

 Oktoberfest began in 1810 when a wedding celebration for Bavarian Prince Ludwig and Princess Theresa turned into a two-week party. Now each year a 16-day festival begins in late September and is celebrated in many places all over the world.

- **Marzenbier** Also called Oktoberfest, Marzen comes from the old custom of brewing beer at the end of the winter so that it will ready for the the end of harvest time in late summer. The beer is stored and cool aged over the summer months. The classic Marzen, a bottom-fermented beer, is a golden yellow, but there is also a dark Marzen.
- **Munich dark and pale** Munich dark (Munchin dunkle) is the old style of Munich beer. Munich, called Munchin in German, claims to be the home of Bavarian brewing. Munchin dark is a bottom-fermented beer that is dark brown in color, and chocolatey, sweet and malty in taste. Munich pale (Munchin helles) is the newer of the two beers, introduced in the 1920s. It is a pale golden color with a sweet malty taste. Both of these beers are moderately low in alcohol content.
- **Pilsner** Today Pilsner or "Pils" is the most popular beer in Germany and is brewed all over the country. Pilsner was first developed in the Bohemia town of Pilsen, in what is now Czechoslovakia. It quickly made its way into Germany and it now commands over 60% of the beer market. It is a pale golden beer that is quite hoppy with a dry finish.

- **Schwartzbier** Translated as "black beer," this type of beer is made in the city of Kulbach. It is one of the few beers in Germany to use roasted malt. The resulting beer is dark, almost black in color. It has a medium body and a malty taste, but is low in sweetness.
- **Rauchbier** This is the "smoke beer." It gets its smokey flavor from the barley that is kilned over a smoldering fire of beechwood. This type of beer has a unique smokey flavor and aroma, with a sweet malty taste.
- **Weissbier** (Weizen) This wheat beer, a top-fermented beer, is also called "white beer." It is made with barley malt and up to 60% wheat malt. Originally brewed in southern Germany, it is usually a pale golden color. Some cloudiness in the beer is acceptable as the wheat protein produces a haze. The filtered variety of this beer, called Kristallweizen, is clear. The unfiltered beer is called Hefeweizen. One characteristic of both of these beers is the thick white foamy head produced when the beer is poured. It is traditional to serve a slice of lemon on the beer glass with these beers.
- **Berliner weisse** This "white beer" can only be brewed in Berlin and is sometimes called the champagne of beers. It is dry, tart, acidy, sour, with fruity undertones. Usually a summer specialty, it is served in bowl-shaped glasses often with raspberry or woodruff syrups to counter the acidic tastes. This is called Weiss mit Schuss. Another variation is Weiss mit Stippe, which is Weiss with caraway schnapps (certainly a different taste sensation!). Berliner weisse has quite a low alcohol content.
- **Weizenbock** This is a wheat bock that is full-bodied and very malty, but low in hops. It is quite strong in alcohol content.

Some breweries in Germany

Brewery	Location	Beers
Becks Brewery Founded 1873 – Germany's largest exporter of beer	Bremen	Beck's Beer, Beck's Dark
Bitburger Brewery Founded 1817	Bitburg	Premium Pils (the number one draught Pilsner in Germany)
Lowenbrau Brewery Founded 1383	Munich	Lowenbrau Premium Pilsner, Munich Dunkel, Munich Helles, Munich Oktoberfest
Spaten-Franziskaner Brewery Founded 1397	Munich	Spaten Premium Lager, Dunkel Export, Spaten Pils, Oktoberfest Optmator Doppelbock Franziskaner Hefe-Weissbier
Ayinger Brewery Founded 1878	Aying	Maibock, Ur Weisse, Celebrator Doppelbock, Oktober-Fest Marzen
Paulaner Salvator Brewery Founded 1634	Munich	Salvator Doppelbock, Munich Dunkel, Premium Pils, Hefe-Weizen
Berliner Kindl Brewery Founded 1872	Berlin	Kindl Weisse, Kindl Pils, Kindl Rauchbier

Dortmunder Actien Brewery (DAB) Founded 1868	Dortmund	DAB Export, DAB Meister Pils
Dortmunder Union Brewery (DUB) Founded 1873	Dortmund	DUB Export, Siegel Pilsner
Einbecker Brewery Founded 1967	Einbeck	Ur Bock Hell, Maibock, Ur Bock Dunkel
Holsten Brewery Founded 1879	Hamburg	Holsten Pils, Holsten Export
Kuppers Kolsch	Cologne	Kuppers Kolsch, Weisse
Schneider Brewery	Kelheim	Schneider Weisse

Belgium

Just imagine: three languages (French, German and Flemish), 10 million people, 150 breweries and 60,000 taverns/cafés (we'd call them pubs). That's one beer outlet for every 170 people! And beers! No other country has the variety of different beers that are found in Belgium. It is no surprise that the average Belgian consumes more than 100 litres of beer per person each year.

Belgian beers are very unique as many of them are only produced in this country. Each of these beers is served in its own unique type of glass. Some Belgian taverns have been known to refuse to serve a certain style of beer because the bar is all out of that particular glass at the moment.

Here are these unique beers:

- **Belgian ales** These are pale ales that are very similar to the British pale ales. Many of them even have British sounding names like Pale Ale and Scottish Ale. They are dark, spicy and hoppy and quite often much stronger than their British counterparts.

- **Belgian red beer** This beer is referred to as the "burgundy of Belgium." It has a dark red color and a sour acidic taste. Belgian red is tart and fruity, but not very hoppy. Reds are quite often aged sometimes as much as two years.
- **Flanders brown ale** Belgian brown ale is copper brown in color. Its characteristics include a sweet and sour taste that is spicy and fruity. There is no hop taste or aroma.
- **Belgian strong ale** This beer can be golden to dark brown in color. The golden ales are top fermented but cold conditioned and medium hopped. The dark ales have a full body and are deep burgundy to brown in color. They have a rich creamy and sweet taste, very little hops and high alcohol content.
- **Trappist ales** (also called Abbey ales) There are only six breweries in the world that can use the name Trappist. Five of these are located in monasteries in Belgium – Westmalle, Orval, Rochefort, Westvleteren and Chimay. The other is located in Schaapskooi in the Netherlands.

  The Abbey beers are generally "dubbel" or "tripel" ales. These terms refer to the density of the beer. The brewer will draw off some of the early wort, which is the heaviest, so that they can make a stronger or double brew. A still stronger beer would be a triple-strength brew. Dubbel ales are 6 to 7.5% ABV, while tripels are 7 to 10% ABV.

Chimay (pronounced "she-may") was the first monastery to commercially brew beer and is the largest of the Trappist brewers today. It started brewing in the 1860s and is credited with introducing the term "Trappist beer." The beer is really produced at the monastery of Notre Dame in the township of Chimay. Three beers, Chimay Red, White and Blue, are made along with the well-known Chimay cheese.

- **Saison** A summer beer that ranges from blonde to coppery orange in color. It has a dense white head and a malty, fruity, tarty taste. Saison is dry-hopped, and then bottle-conditioned as additional yeast is added to the bottle.
- **Lambics** Lambics are only brewed in Belgium. They are also called the "wild beers" because they are fermented naturally by airborne yeast. This process is called "spontaneous fermentation." Lambics are wheat beers that are brewed with about 30% wheat added to the barley malt. All lambics have a sour, acidic, fruity taste. The three most common lambics are:
  Fruit lambics Made from a lambic base, these beers are dry and champagne-like. They have a cloudy, hazy appearance with a sour taste. There is little hops aroma or taste. The two most popular fruit lambics are kriek (cherry-flavored) and framboise (raspberry-flavored).
  Gueuze This beer is a blend of young and old lambics. It is conditioned for six to nine months, but can be laid down for as long as five years. Gueuze has a sharp tart, acidic taste, but is not bitter. Its color deepens with age from gold to amber.
  Faro One of the oldest lambics, faro has rock sugar added to create a sweet-sour taste. It is a cloudy yellow in color.

  Most lambics are served on draft in Belgium; only a few are bottled. As a result the availability of these beers is limited outside the country.
- **Witbier** (White beer) This is a beer much like Berliner weisse but stronger and maltier. It has a pale hazy yellow color and a white head, which is normal for wheat beers. Witbier is mildly sweet, malty, spicy and fruity. It is medium-hopped with a medium body and a dry finish.
- **Pilsner** Not to be lost in the shuffle, Belgium does produce many fine Pilsners. These beers are regarded as everyday beers by Belgians. Most Pilsners are dry, well-hopped, with a clean finish.

Sour beer?

Many of the beers produced in Belgian have been described
as sour or tart. This is particularly true of the lambics. A novice
would no doubt be startled at his first taste of one of these
beers. But hang in there: Belgian beers are an acquired taste
that just takes a few moments. Then you'll discover how the
brewers have balanced out the sourness with a sweet side,
giving the beer a smooth, dry finish. Definitely different, but
very satisfying.

Some breweries in Belgium

Brewery	Location	Beers
Notre Dame Abbey Founded 1862 The best-known – of the five Trappist breweries in Belgium	Chimay	Chimay Rouge, Chimay Blanche ("tripel" ale 8% ABV), Chimay Bleu (strong beer 9% ABV)
Brouwerij Liefmans Founded 1679	Oudenaard	Oud Bruin, Goudenband, Kriekbier, Frambozenbier
Brouwerij Moortgat Founded 1871	Breendonk	Duval, Maredsous 6, 8, 10
Notre Dame Abbey de St. Remy Founded 1899	Rochefort Trappist abbey	Rochefort 6, 8, 10
Abbey De Notre Dame Founded 1931	Orval	Orval Trappist Ale

Abbey St. Sixtus	Westvleteren	Special 6, Extra 8,
Founded 1839		Abt 12
– smallest of the Trappist abbeys		
Trappist Abbey	Malle	Westmalle "tripel",
de Westmalle		Westmalle Dubbel
Belle-Vue	Brussels	Kriek,
Founded 1913		Framboise
– Belgium's largest brewer of lambics		
Brouwerij Bosteels	Buggenhout	Pauwel Kwak, Kwak,
Founded 1791		Prosit Pils
Brouwerij de Kluis	Hoegaarden	Hoegaarden Witbier
Founded 1966		Julius, Grand Cru,
		Verboden Vrucht
Brouwerij	Vlezenbeek	Framboise, Kriek,
Lindemans		Gueuze
Founded 1869		
Brouwerij	Roeselare	Belgian Red Ale,
Rodenbach		Grand Cru
Founded 1836		
Brouwerij Artois	Leuven	Stella Artois Pilsner (Belgium's number one lager)
Brouwerijen	Waarloos	Maes Pils,
Alken Maes		Cristal Pils,
Founded 1988		Grimbergen Abbey Ales

CZECH REPUBLIC

The Czechs pride themselves as the world's greatest beer drinkers, averaging over 160 litres of beer per person per year. The central brewing region is in Bohemia with three great brewing districts of Prague, Pilzen (Pilsner) and Ceske Budejovice.

In 1842, a new beer was introduced in Pilzen, Bohemia. It was a bottom-fermenting brew that was golden yellow in color, highly hopped and very refreshing when served cold. Pilsen gave its name to this new style of beer and soon it became very popular everywhere in the country. By the 1850s Pilsner was being exported and soon the recipe was copied by brewers all over the world. It is now called Pils, Pilsener or Pilzensky. It is in Pilsen that the famous Pilsner Urquell is brewed. The name derives from "ur," which means original. This beer is clear, golden, crisp and quite hoppy and is considered by many to be the gold standard of all Pilsners.

All of the lager beers produced in North America are loosely based on this style, but the taste really isn't all that similar. The American brewers decided that their beers would be more popular with the masses if they de-hopped them, creating less bite and eventually a lot less flavor.

In Ceske Budejovice the best-known beer is called Budweiser. It is called the "Original Budweiser" by its brewers since it was being brewed long before its more famous American counterpart. The only problem with the Budvar claim to originality is that the present-day Budvar brewery did not open until 1895, 20 years after Anheuser-Busch had started brewing their "Bud" in St. Louis. Interestingly, Anheuser-Busch also brews Michelob, which is named after another town in Bohemia.

Some breweries in the Czech Republic

Brewery	Location	Beers
Pilsner Urquell Founded 1842	Pilzen	Pilsner Urquell, Gambrinus 12, Primus
Budweiser	Budejovice	Budweiser Budejovice BudvarCeske

| **U Fleka** | Prague | Flekovsky Lezek |

Founded 1499
– Claims to be the oldest brewery in the world

| **Staropramen** | Prague | Staropramen Lager, |

Founded 1869 — Staropramen Dark

DENMARK

The Danes are quite high on the beer consumption scale, drinking over 122 litres per person a year. This is the fourth highest consumption level in the world.

Carlsberg, one of the most famous breweries worldwide, controls the brewing industry in Denmark. It has a market share of around 80%. Carlsberg is part of the Carlsberg A/S group, which includes the Carlsberg, Frederika, Neptune, Wilbroes and Tuborg breweries. Recently, it merged with the British Allied-Tetley to form one of the largest brewing companies in the world.

Carlsberg was founded by Jacob Christian Jacobsen in 1874. Jacobsen took a scientific approach to his brewing, following the principles set out by his good friend Louis Pasteur. He set up the Carlsberg Laboratories, which took a great interest in studying the brewing sciences. One of these scientists was Emil Christian Hanson who isolated the first single cell yeast culture in 1883. This discovery enabled brewers to have a more consistent yeast strain and eliminated many of the bad beer batches that where all too common.

Carlsberg now brews in nine countries, licenses in 14 and exports their beer to more than 100 countries around the world. Their initial beer, Carlsberg Pilsner was a Pilsner-style beer that became popular in the mid-1800s. The everyday beer for most of Denmark, Carlsberg Pilsner is malty, highly hopped and very refreshing.

Tuborg produces a premium Pilsner lager that is drier and hoppier than Carlsberg. Its brewing branch also brews a wide selection of other beers for the Danish market.

As a step into the future, Carlsberg, innovative as always, is bringing out the world's first refillable plastic beer bottle for both their Carlsberg and Tuborg brands.

Some breweries in Denmark

Brewery	Location	Beers
Carlsberg Brewery Founded 1847	Copenhagen	Carlsberg Pilsner, Elephant Beer, Carlsberg Dark, Imperial Stout
Tuborg Brewery Founded 1873	Copenhagen	Tuborg Pilsner Gold, Porter
Albani Brewery Founded 1859	Odense	Giraf Lager, Albani Pilsner
Faxe Brewery	Faske	Faxe Premium Pils

THE NETHERLANDS

The Netherlands brewing scene is dominated by Heineken, perhaps the best-known beer in the world. Heineken produces its beers in over 90 breweries in 50 countries around the world. The brewery was founded in 1864 by Gerard Adriaan Heineken in the city of Amsterdam. Heineken also owns the Amstel brewery, named after the Amstel River that flows through Amsterdam. For the Dutch the everyday beer or Pils is the internationally known Heineken Pilsner. This is a light, fruity and effervescent beer.

In the 1950s Grolsch decided to phase out their "old-fashioned" bottle but were met with extreme opposition. Grolsch kept their recognized bottle and, as a result, it has become one of the best-known beer containers in the world. It has been called "a good Pilsner-style beer in a great bottle." This bottle is also very popular with the homebrewers who find it an easy way to package their homebrew.

Grolsch, the beer with the famous ceramic swing-top bottle stopper, also brews a full line of beers. Their best-known beer is Grolsch Pilsner bottled in the celebrated green bottle.

Some breweries in the Netherlands

Brewery	Location	Beers
Heinken Founded 1863	Amsterdam	Heinken, Tarwebok, Von Vollenhoeven Stout, Kylian, Amstel Lager
Schaapskooi Abbey Founded 1884 – the only Trappist Abbey brewery outside of Belgium	Koningshoeven	Trappist Ales, Dubbel "tripel", Quadrupel (all of these are sold under La Trappe and Koningshoeven labels)
Oranjeboom Brewery Founded 1670	Breda	Oranjeboom Pils, Oranjeboom Oud Bruin

FRANCE

It is no surprise to learn that beer is not the number one drink in France. The French, with just a 39 litres per capita yearly consumption, are the second-lowest beer-drinking country in Europe. (Only Italy is lower than France with a 25 litres rate.) Beer is more popular in the northern regions of the country where the influence of Belgium is more apparent.

But the French do love their brasseries and they do have their own unique beer style. This is called *biere en garde*, which means "beer to keep." This style is a top-fermented beer that is similar to the Belgian ales. The beer is dark amber in color, malty, full-bodied and usually corked like wine. The brewers use several malts to get their unique tastes. After bottling, the beer is laid down for a few months to mature.

The most popular style of beer in France is Pilsner. Here Kronenbourg, the largest brewing company in France, is king. This brewery's regular beer, Kronenbourg, is your standard light European lager. They also produce Kronebourg 1664, a premium beer which is a fuller more substantial brew.

Another unique French beer is the Bière de Paris, once known as "Paris brown." It is much like *bière en garde*, but is a lager. It is a dark, strong beer that is bottled with a cork. While it is true that beer is not as prevalent as wine in France, its popularity in recent years is growing. As in countries all over the world, many microbreweries have sprung up in France, producing world-style beers like wheat beer, real ale and several new *biere en garde* styles for new-generation beer drinkers.

Some breweries in France

Brewery	Location	Beers
Brasserie St. Sylvestre Founded 1918	St. Sylvestre-Cappel	Trois Monts *(biere en garde)* Grand Reserve, Biere de Noel, Biere de Mars
Brasserie Castlain Founded 1966	Benifountaine	Ch'ti Blonde, Ch'Amber, Ch'ti Bruin (all *bieres en garde*)
Brasserie Duyck Founded 1922	Jenlain	Jenlain *(biere en garde)*, Sebourg Blonde
Brasseries Kronenbourg Founded 1664 France's biggest brewer	Strasbourg	Kronenbourg (which has about 25% of the beer market), Kronenbourg 1664 (the premium lager)

AUSTRIA

Austria is one the more active beer-drinking nations with a per capita consumption of 115 litres per year. Austrians don't drink as much beer as the Germans and they certainly do not have the variety of beer styles found in Germany, but they did originate one of the world's classic beers styles, Vienna lager. In 1841 Anton Dreher introduced this style to the people of Vienna. It was a reddish, amber, bottom-fermenting beer that had a distinct malty taste. The style has all but disappeared in Austria but is now a very popular beer in Mexico and the southwestern United States.

There are more than 70 breweries making beer in Austria. They brew Pilsner, weissbier and bock beers. As well, the old Vienna beer has been revived by many of the new microbreweries.

Some breweries in Austria

Brewery	Location	Beers
Eggenberg Brewery Founded 1681	Vorchdorf	Urbock 23, MacQueen's Nessie, Eggenberg Marzen, Hopfen Konig
Weiselberg Brewery Founded 1770	Weiselberg	Weiselberger Gold, Weiselberger Stammbrau
Ottakringer Brewery Founded 1837	Vienna	Vienna-styled lagers, Gold Fassel

ITALY

As with their French neighbors, wine is much more popular with Italians than beer. With the lowest beer consumption rate in Europe (25 litres per person per year), it is surprising that several of Italy's beers are well known in North America. Moretti brews beer in northern Italy close to the Austrian border. Its two famous beers are Moretti Pilsner and La Rossa Double Malt. All of Moretti's brands bear the distinctive picture of the moustached man, which is certainly not John Labatt of Canada, whose company recently took over control of this brewery.

The largest brewery in Italy is Birra Peroni, with six breweries in operation all over the country. Their brands include: Peroni, Nastro Azzurro, Itala Pilsen, Raffo and Crystall Simplon.

NORWAY

Like several of the other Scandinavian counties, Norway's beers are not very well known outside the home country, but there are a few national brands. The government has put strict controls on the production of beer in Norway and applied high taxes to any alcoholic beverages. This may or may not discourage drinking, but it does tend to hurt exports.

Some breweries in Norway

Brewery	Location	Beers
Aass Bryggeri (pronounced ohss) Founded 1834	Drammen	Aass Bock, Jule Ø1, Aass Amber
Hansa Bryggeri Founded 1890	Bergen	Hansa Premium Pilsner, Hansa Bayer, Hansa Export Ø1
Ringes Bryggeri Founded 1877	Oslo	Rignes Pilsner Beer, Special Bock, Christmas Ale, Frydenlund Pilsner

SWEDEN

As in Norway, the Swedish government has strict control of the beer industry and there are only a limited number of breweries in the country.

Some breweries in Sweden

Brewery	Location	Beers
Pripps Bryggeri Founded 1828 – Largest brewery in Sweden	Stockholm	Pripps Bla (Blue), Carnegie Porter,

Spendrups Bryggeri Stockholm   Spendrups Original,
Founded 1859   Norrlands Gold

FINLAND

With the exception of the Danes, the Finns drink more beer than the other Scandinavians. They consume around 80 litres per capita per year.

Finnish beer is classified by strength rather than by style. Class I beers, called table beers or Kalja, are low in alcohol (2.8% ABV or less). Class II beers no longer exist because they were not very popular. Class III beers, also called supermarket beers, are the most common and the most popular beers in Finland (4 to 4.8% ABV). Class IV beers are the strongest (4.9 to 5.6% ABV) and the most heavily taxed. There is also a Class IVB that includes the higher-alcohol malt liquors. This is a rather confusing system but one common to all Scandinavian countries.

FINLAND

Some breweries in Finland

Brewery	Location	Beers
Hartwell Brewery Founded 1873	Helsinki	Lapin Kulta, Weizenfest
Sinebrychoff Brewery Founded 1819	Kerava	Koff Export, Koff Porter, Koff Strong

Sahti, the traditional Finnish beer

Sahti is a very old style of beer that is made only in Finland. Traditionally it is created from rye hops, yeast and traditional berries. This is a homebrew beer recipe that is cooked over an open fire all day. The mash is then filtered through juniper branches and straw, and then fermented for about a week. The traditional alcohol content is very strong (around 12% ABV). Today Sahti is produced commercially by micro-breweries and brew pubs but the commercial alcohol content of 5% ABV is much lower.

BREWING IN THE REST OF EUROPE

Virtually every country in Europe now brews its own beers. Most of these are not exported. Here are some of the highlights just in case you go travelling:

Some breweries in the rest of Europe

Brewery	Location	Beers
Okocim Browar	Poland	Okocim Pils, Porter
Zywiec Browar	Poland	Zyweic Pilsner, Porter
Kobanyai Sorgyar	Budapest	Dreher Pils, Export
San Miguel	Spain	Pale Pilsner
Damm	Barcelona, Spain	Vol Damm, Bock Damm
El Aguila	Madrid, Spain	Aguila Pilsner, Reserve

Ten world beers that you should try

Not necessarily the world's top 10 beers but a good selection of interesting beers.

- **Guinness Extra Stout** Guinness Brewing, Dublin, Ireland. Undoubtedly the world's best stout. A creamy perfectly balanced beer. The draft, made domestically, is not as good as the Guinness in Ireland. The canned variety, with the foam-producing widget, is pretty close to the original.
- **Pilsner Urquell** Pilzen, Czechoslovakia. *Urquell* means "original." This is the beer that all the rest of the world styles their lagers after. Pale gold in color, with hops and malt balanced perfectly. A wonderful lip-smacking finish.
- **Lindemans Cuvée René** A lambic gueuze. Unlike any other beer style that you'll ever taste.
- **Newcastle Brown Ale** The perfect brown ale. Sweet, smooth with a hint of caramel. Best out of the distinctive clear bottle, or so the locals say.
- **Bass Ale** Bass Brewers, Burton-on-Trent, England. The classic India pale ale.
- **Anchor Steam Beer** Anchor Brewing, San Francisco, California. A truly unique American beer, made with lager yeast and then fermented warm like an ale. This is an original – fruity, hoppy, well balanced.
- **Fuller's London Pride** A classic British bitter.
- **Chimay Rouge** A Trappist dubbel ale, strong, fruity, spicy. The other Chimay beers are Chimay Blanc and Chimay Bleu.
- **Pete's Wicked Ale** A good American Brown Ale.
- **Bitburger Premium Pils** The perfect example of a German Pils, light, dry and hoppy.

CHAPTER SEVEN

Brewing in
the rest of the world

CENTRAL AMERICA, SOUTH AMERICA AND THE CARIBBEAN

Beer brewing on this continent can be traced back to the time of the Aztecs. Records show that they brewed a beer made from tree sap and maize. A similar type of beer was produced by the Incas of Peru, and both tribes referred to this beer as *chicha*. This style of beer is still being made by the local natives in their villages. As in ancient times, it is consumed through a straw. Chichas range in color from a pale yellow to a dark red due the degree of maize and other grains used in the brewing process. The other common beer was called *masato*, which was made from the Manioc tuber. It is usually milky white and very thick.

Today the most popular beers are those based on the European lager style. This is, of course, the same all over the world since about 90% of the beer brewed in the world is a lager product.

Mexico

The Mexican beer market is dominated by FEMSA. It owns nine breweries around the country including the Cerveceria Cuauhtemoc and the Cerveceria Moctezuma. Their brands include Carta Blanca, Indio, Bohemia, Chihuahua, Tecate, Dos Equis, Tres Equis, Superior and Sol. In 1994 Labatt's bought into this large Mexican company.

Dos Equis XXX is perhaps the best known of the Mexican Vienna-style beers. Vienna-style dark lagers were brought over to Mexico in the 1860s when the Austrian Maximilian took over as Emperor of Mexico and the country was incorporated into the Austrian Empire. Maximilian didn't last long (he was soon overthrown and executed), but the beer style remained as a Mexican staple. This type of beer has a full-bodied malty flavor with a strong hoppy finish, and it suits the spicy Mexican cuisine.

In **Brazil** the indigenous peoples used to make a black beer, using roots and local grains that were cooked over open fires. This style of beer, called Todat, remains in some parts of Brazil. Again, the truly popular beers are the locally made lagers.

In the **Caribbean**, golden lagers predominate, but the influence of the British Empire is obvious as the second most popular beers are the stouts.

Some Breweries in Central America, South America and the Caribbean:

Brewery	Location	Beers
Cerveceria Moctezuma & Cerveceria Cuauhtemoc	Monterrey, Mexico	Dos Equis, Carta Blanca, Sol, Bohemia, Tecate, Superior, Tres Equis Indio
Cerveceria Modelo	Mexico City Mexico	Corona, Negra Modelo, Negra Leon
Cerveceria Biekert	Buenos Aries, Argentina	Biekert Pisner Cerveza
Cerveceria Polar	Caracas, Venezuela	Polar Lager
Cervejarie Cacdor	Brazil	Xingu Black Beer

Companhia Brahma	Brazil	Brahma Pilsner
Desnoes & Geddes	Kingston, Jamaica	Dragon Stout, Red Stripe
Banks Breweries	Barbados	Banks Lager
Caribe Brewery	Trinidad	Caribe Lager

ASIA

China

The history of brewing beer in China dates back thousands of years. Lager-styles beers were introduced in the 1800s by Western traders. In 1897 a group of German brewers opened the **Tsingtao** brewery. Now nationally owned, it is China's most famous and most popular beer, holding 22% of the Chinese beer market.

The Chinese do not consume much beer (12.5 litres per person a year) but because of the large population, China's overall beer production is quite high. Beer is now the cheapest drink in the country outside water. Unfortunately the quality of the local products is inconsistent.

American and European breweries are a huge presence on the Chinese beer market. Budweiser, Pabst, Beck's, Carlsberg, Heineken and San Miguel (it's actually from the Philippines) are all trying to gain a piece of the gigantic market available in China. In fact, Pabst, the number one Western-style beer in China, has recently entered into a new agreement and will open several new breweries. Lion Nathan, the giant Australian conglomerate, presently owns two breweries in China.

Chui is the name of a wheat beer made more than 200 ago in China. Now chui is the generic term for beer in most of the country.

There are over 100 breweries making beer in China today. Some popular local beers are Zhujiang, Beijing and Taihushui.

Japan

As with China, beer has been produced in Japan for a long time. Three major breweries control the beer market in Japan:

- **Kirin** is the number one brewery in the country. Established in 1870 by an American named William Copeland, the brewery now makes a full range of beers including lagers, dark ales and stouts. Today the Japanese-owned brewery exports its number one beer, Kirin, all over the world.

- **Asahi** is the second largest brewer in Japan. It operates seven breweries all over Japan. The best-known beer produced by Asahi is their Asahi Dry. Other products are: Asahi Pure Gold, Asahi Draught, Asahi Super Premium, Asahi Original 6. This company also brews Coors under license.

- **Sapporo** Founded in 1876, Sapporo was the first Japanese-owned brewery. Now the third largest brewery in Japan, it's brews include Sapporo Draft, Sapporo Black Beer and Yebisu Premium

Asahi Super Dry

In 1987 Asahi introduced a new beer to the market. Their idea was to make a beer that had a strong initial taste or effect. The brewers were able to brew out the finish, creating a beer with almost no aftertaste. The new beer was an instant hit in Japan and soon Kirin copied it, bringing out their own version called Kirin Dry. By the late 1980s. Dry beer was the most popular beer style in Japan. This new beer fad quickly spread to the United States and Canada, and soon almost every brewing company had their own "dry" brand.

The rest of the Asian countries are not big consumers of beer but most have breweries and the odd one even produces a memorable beer.

Thailand is noted for its **Singha** and **Klosters**.

The once-famous **Tiger Lager** is brewed in **Singapore**. It is described as a dry, hoppy beer. During WWII the British troops stationed in Singapore made it a well-known beer. The brewery also makes **Tiger Stout**.

In **Saigon, Vietnam "33" Export** was the most popular beer with American troops.

In India the biggest beer maker is the United Brewery group. This company makes the well-known **Kingfisher Lager** as well.

San Miguel, one of the more famous breweries in Asia, is located in the Philippines. It has been brewing since the late 1800s and recently sold its brewery interests in Spain. **San Miguel Lager** is one of the better beers made in Asia.

AFRICA

The brewing of beer in Africa dates back thousands of years to the ancient Egyptians who left extensive records of their beer creations. Researchers have also discovered that tribes in interior Africa made beer in their villages. These beers were made from whatever grains or grasses were available to them. The ancient African beers were sour, porridge-like and often consumed through long reed straws.

Due to religious restrictions, there are no longer brewers in Moslem Egypt, but most other African countries are actively brewing beer.

In **South Africa**, the brewing market is dominated by South African Breweries, which is a conglomerate of several breweries. Their brands include Castle Lager, Lion Lager, Hansa, Fraisen St. Wheat Beer and Ohlssons.

In **Nigeria**, Guinness is one of the dominant breweries. Local laws state that any brewery must brew a special recipe not brewed by Guinness anywhere else in the world. As a result, the four Nigerian Guinness breweries produce some very unique products. In addition, Nigeria has over 30 other breweries, making it one of Africa's larger brewing nations.

Kenya is home to another very famous beer, Tusker. This beer is exported internationally.

Tanzania produces some very good lagers such as Kilimanjaro, Serengeti, Ndova, Castle and Safari.

Namibia's beer brands include Windhock, Holstein, Tafel and Urbock.

The most popular beer in **Zimbabwe** is Zambezi.

NEW ZEALAND

Captain James Cook is credited with brewing the first beer in New Zealand. In 1773 he arrived at these islands and ordered a brew of native leaves and molasses as a drink to help stave off scurvy for his sailors.

Today New Zealand has two national breweries and 60 other regional and microbreweries producing 230 local beers.

The national breweries are:

- **Lion Breweries, Auckland.**

This brewery is part of the giant Lion Nathan Company. It took over the national New Zealand Brewery in 1977. There are three Lion Breweries around the country. Local brands include Lion Red Lion Brown, Lion Light, Lion Ice, Leopard Black Label, Speights, Waikato Bitter and Canterbury Draught Steinlager.

In the late 1950s Lion Breweries introduced a new lager to New Zealand. It was a premium beer that was based on the finest lagers brewed in Europe. The recipe produced a crisp, Pilsner-styled beer. The beer was originally called Steinecker because in Germany beer is consumed in drinking vessels called steins. At first this beer came in a brown pint bottle. In 1962 the name was changed to Steinlager and the beer was marketed internationally. Starting in the late 1970s the Steinlager bottle was changed to the distinctive green one known today. At the moment Steinlager is by far New Zealand's largest exported beer with 94% of the export market.

- **Dominion Breweries (DB).**

The second largest brewery in New Zealand has four brewing sites. Its brews include: DB Draught, DB Bitter, DB Export Gold, DB Dry Lager, Tui's.

AUSTRALIA

Australia is a big country with a considerable reputation for its massive beer consumption. In truth, Australians rank tenth in the world with an approximate consumption of 98 litres of beer per person each year. The Down Under beer market is dominated by the Pilsner-style lagers. Originally Australia's breweries were all regional. Each of the six states had its own breweries and rarely exported to another state. Even today, the breweries are state-based, but most are owned by larger brewing conglomerates.

Beer drinking is one of the favorite pastimes of many Australians. Most of the beer is served very cold hence the beer terms "coldie" or "frostie." Since most of the beer consumed is of the draft variety, it is important to know how to order a beer down in "Oz." In most places if you want a large glass of beer you would ask for a "schooner." A smaller glass is called a "middie."

Here are some Australian breweries divided according to their state of origin.

- **Victoria** Home of the best-known Australian beer, Foster's. Founded in 1888, it is recognized internationally as a symbol of Australia brewing but it isn't really the beer of the country. Foster's is part of Carlton & United, which also owns the Abbotts, Brisbane, Carlton, Resch and Victoria and Sheaf brewing operations. Foster's is brewed in eight countries and marketed in 120 countries all over the world. Its two main products are Foster's Lager and Foster's Special Bitter. Foster's is also brewed in New South Wales. Other notable beers are Sheaf Stout and Victoria Bitter.

- **New South Wales** This residents of this state have the reputation for consuming more beer than any of the other Australian states. One of the few remaining local breweries is Tooheys, now owned by the giant Lion Nathan but still producing some noteworthy beers.

- **South Australia** Cooper's is the only remaining family-owned large brewery in Australia. It was founded in 1862 by Thomas Cooper and still produces traditional beers that are unlike most of the breweries in Australia. Many of its beers are bottle-conditioned. Some Cooper's brands include: Real Ale, Exotic Stout Big Barrel Lager and Sparkling Ale (which isn't sparkling at all but just the opposite, cloudy, with sediment on the bottom).

- **Queensland** This state is home to Castlemaine, another one of the better-known Australian beers. Castlemaine XXXX Lager is exported all over the world. Some of the other well-received brews are XXXX Gold, XXXX Bitter and Carbine Stout. Castlemaine is owned by Lion Nathan.

- **Tasmania** This island state has two very good breweries, Cascade and Boags. Cascade was founded in 1824 and is Australia's oldest brewery, producing a sparkling lager and a stout. Boags is a famous brewery that brews Boags Draught, XXX Ale and Stout.
- **Western Australia** The Swan Brewery was one of the first Australian breweries to market their beer abroad. It is now owned by Lion Nathan, located in Perth, and produces Swan Lager, Gold, Light, Export and Stout Swan also brews the Emu brands of beer.

CHAPTER EIGHT

Buying, serving and evaluating beer

Twenty-four beers in a case,
twenty-four hours in a day – coincidence?
—Stephen Wright

People don't walk into a restaurant and simply ask for food, they're specific. Some people prefer a fairly bland diet while others seek exotic dishes to challenge their palate. Either way you don't want to eat the same meal every day.

The same can be said for the beer that you consume. Many swear allegiance to "their brand," perhaps because they want no surprises and can expect a taste that they enjoy. But these people, just like a person who eats the same food every day, are missing a great deal. Just as there are everyday wines and vintage wines, so there are many choices in beer – all worth tasting.

- **Beer and bread** A useful analogy is to compare beer to bread (actually not a bad idea since they both are made from the same sort of grain). The big-mass, produced beers can be seen as generic sliced white bread. Both are consistent in quality, not very exciting and difficult to differentiate one from another.

  Of course, there are a lot of other breads out there: rye, pumpernickel, Italian, French, jalapeno and whole wheat, just to name a few. Many of these breads are more expensive and most of us understand that's because of the ingredients and baking processes. Like "premium" bread, premium and microbrewed beers are more expensive than the regular or popular priced beers because there's more in them.

The taste test

Try blind tasting a group of similar Canadian or American beers. (Don't mix them because Canadian beers generally have more body than their American counterparts.) Make sure that they are all are the same type of beer such as Labatt Blue, Molson Canadian, Carling Lager and a Kokanee. Or try Budweiser, Miller, Pabst and an Old Milwaukee. You will probably have difficulty distinguishing one beer from another. In fact you may not be able to pick your own favorite brand from the others.

Okay, what beer do I order (or pick off the shelf)?

As we already know, there is a great variety of beers out there. In fact, there is probably a different style of beer for each occasion. Each separate moment, mood, even meal could call for a different style of beer.

If you're new to the game, start out with the Pilsner-style beers. After all, they are by far the most popular and most common beers to find. Certainly the European Pilsners taste quite a bit different from those brewed locally, but it's not necessary to start with these expensive imports. There are many craft-brewed lagers that taste identical to expensive imported beers.

If you are more adventurous and would like to try the other beer styles, but unsure how to go about it, why not think seasonally? *Many of the different beer styles were brewed with a season in mind.*

Summer	**Examples**
This is a time for a beer that will quench your thirst: a drink that should be served cold, but not iced so that it will kill your tastebuds.	Pilsners, wheat beers, Canadian/American lagers, pale ales, Witbier, Weissbier, Saison

Spring/Fall

Certain beers were traditionally brewed for celebrations like Easter and Oktoberfest. These beers are medium- to full-bodied and are quite malty.

Bock beers, Oktoberfest/Marzen beers, Vienna dark lagers

Winter

The colder months lend themselves to heavier beers. These are usually much darker and very full-bodied.

Doppelbock, tripelbock, Scottish and Irish ales, Belgian Strong ales, Trappist ales, Special winter beers

This is just a guide to get started. You can certainly enjoy any of these beers anytime of the year.

How can I find different beers?

The answer is quite simple – look at the labels, front and back. All beer sold in Canada must indicate the type of beer, the alcohol content, the volume of the container and quite often the brewer. The microbrews and imported beers will often have a back label with a brief description of their beer and sometimes their brewery. Most will have a "best before" date or a brew date (when the beer was made).

Additives?

Many of the European beers have the Reinheitsgebot statement on their labels, indicating the ingredients used, but often the ingredients are not listed. This especially true of Canadian and American beers in spite of the great many additives allowed in the production of beer in this country. The Canadian Food and Drug Act allows 105 different additives in beer brewing. Most of these are preservatives, stabilizers, foam enhancers, and so on. All of these are believed to help in modern-day brewing. Of course none of these additives seem to be harmful, but are they really necessary?

Cans or draft or bottles, it's our favorite brew
(Line from a song promoting Carling Red Cap in the 1960s.)

Today beer is available in cans, bottles and kegs. Not all beer is available in cans or at your local pub.

- **Glass beer bottles** have been around for about 400 years. Today beer is normally bottled in one of three different colors of glass: brown, green and clear. Clear and green glass does not offer much protection from the harmful rays of the sun. Beer affected by the sun is said to be "light struck" or skunky. Light-colored beers like lagers are especially susceptible to the light. Brown glass offers protection from the light.
- **Cans,** which were introduced in the United States in 1935, revolutionized the beer business. People went from drinking draft in their favorite tavern or pub to buying it and bringing it home to consume. Of course there were still bottles, but they didn't offer the advantages of cans. Beer cans could be cooled faster and were lighter and more convenient than bottles.

At first the cans occasionally gave a "tinny" taste to the beer. Then a synthetic liner was invented to separate the beer from the can. Eventually Coors, in the early 1950s, introduced the aluminum can. Nowadays canned and bottled beer should taste the same.

In many areas of Canada, cans are more expensive than bottles. It seems that the provincial governments decided that they would raise taxes on canned beer to the prevent beer can pollution.

But did you ever notice that a beer can contains 14 mL more beer than a bottle?

- **Kegs** The other way to get your beer is in a keg. Of course pubs do serve their draft beer from kegs. Keg beer is usually unpasteurized and, for many, tastes better than the stuff you get in bottles or cans. But the imported draft that you order in your pub is probably pasteurized because it wouldn't survive the journey unpasteurized. That is why your pint of expensive, British draft beer doesn't taste as good as it would at its point of origin.

Draft or draught?

Draft is the North American spelling of the British term "draught." Originally draught referred to the draught horses that pulled the wagon that delivered the beer to the pubs or taverns. Draft beer is pumped out of the kegs (sometimes called casks), either by a mixture of pressurized carbon dioxide and nitrogen or by hand pull.

Hand pulls are very popular in Britain where the pubs serve traditional real ale. More recently they have become popular with the outlets serving microbrewed ales in North America.

Draft beer is not just available in pubs – you can get your own keg of beer as well. Of course you probably need to throw a party in order to consume the beer quickly enough. Draft beer in kegs does not have a long life after it has been tapped.

Why get a keg?

Advantages of beer in kegs:

- better tasting
- great for a party – less cleanup afterwards
- about 25% cheaper than buying bottles or cans

Many of the smaller breweries also offer keg service but you better make sure that your guests will like the beer being served or else you'll have a lot left over.

Disadvantages of beer in kegs

- The first couple of pulls will be a little foamy, so there is a bit of waste at the start.
- It's quite possible that you will have leftover beer. A lot left over negates the cheaper beer price since the beer will soon go off.
- Beer kegs are heavy. The smaller keg is not too unwieldy but certainly weighs more than your average 24. You'll need help with the larger one.

Contract brewing

Some of the very popular unique beers found at your local beer outlet are contract-brewed by one of the larger brewing companies. In Ontario Dave's beers, which have an very unique list of brands, are brewed by Molson's. The big national brewery is given the recipe desired by the contractor and brews the beer in smaller batches than its major brews. There is of course nothing wrong with this. The quality is very consistent and many different styles of beer, not normally brewed by the big brewery, are offered under contract.

Beer under license

In Canada both of the "Big Two" breweries and many of the regional brewers offer well-known international beers that are brewed in Canada. While all of these brews are made according to an original recipe, too often they don't taste much like the original. Different ingredients might have to be used by the brewer and quite often the recipe is altered to what the brewery thinks are "Canadian tastes."

Beer storage

The shelf life of beer is about three months. This could be decreased by storage in warm temperatures or direct exposure to daylight. Beer is best stored at around 8° to 13°C.

SERVING AND TASTING BEER

For the most part, beer is served far too cold in North America. The term "ice-cold beer" will strike horror in the heart of a true beer lover. Cold beer would not only numb your palate but it keeps the true taste of the beer locked up.

The average refrigerator temperature is around 4°C (just under 40°F). A beer taken out of the refrigerator and served immediately will not show any of the beer's tastes or flavors. Of course if it is a bland beer, then perhaps this is the only way to serve it.

Proper serving temperature

Light lagers (Pilsners)	5° to 9°C
Dark/amber lagers	8° to 10°C
Pale ales	8° to 10°C
Dark ale and stouts	10° to 13°C

(British cellar temperatures!)

What do you do with a beer that is served too cold? Let it stand for a minute or so – it'll gradually warm up. Drinking beer at the proper temperature will allow you to really taste the flavor and ingredients.

What am I tasting?

Good beers are usually made from just-malted barley, hops, yeast and water (remember the Reinheitsgebot?). You should be able to taste these in a balanced fashion.

Here are some things that even the most inexperienced beer taster should be able to pick up.

- **Hoppiness** Obviously produced by the addition of hops during the brewing process. Hops give a bitter taste that is quite distinctive: sometimes very pronounced, sometimes subtle.

- **Maltiness** A sweet flavor that comes from the malted barley used in the brewing. Sometimes only one malt is used, sometimes several. If the malt is roasted, it will give a richer or stronger effect. These can produce flavors described as nutty, toasty, chocolatey, coffee-like. Again the maltiness may be very strong or not present at all.

- **Body** This is the mouth feel. It can range from very light to heavy. Lager beer could be described as light-bodied, ales as medium-bodied and stouts as full-bodied.

- **Carbonation** This is the effervescence of the beer. Lagers tend to more bubbly than ales.

- **Yeast effects** (from fermentation) This process is responsible for some of the other characteristics of beer. Ales can have a fruity, buttery, sometimes butterscotch taste. Lagers do not have any of these tastes. Fermentation also produces the alcohol taste, which should be apparent only in the very strong beers.

- **Aftertaste** (the finish) That lingering flavor left from that last sip. If it is a good aftertaste it will lead to another sip. Some beers (light, ice and dry) have little or no aftertaste. Good beers have a wonderful finish that can only be experienced directly.

FOR SERIOUS TASTING

Hint #1 Pour the beer into a glass. In fact, pour it into a glass that will take the entire contents of the bottle. Pouring releases the carbonation. If the carbonation isn't released, then the carbon dioxide is trapped in the bottle. When you drink, the gas goes straight to your stomach and may struggle to release itself – burp!

Another reason for pouring is that when the carbon dioxide is released, the aroma and flavor of the beer are also released.

Hint #2 Pour the beer the proper way. How much you tilt the glass as you pour the beer depends on the type of beer. Practice makes perfect here. When you are finished you should have about one inch of head on your beer. The perfect glass of beer boasts a rich head of foam, a natural cap for the beer's carbonation.

Hint #3 Serve at the right temperature. The colder the beer is, the less carbon dioxide is released. The less carbon dioxide released, the fewer flavors and aroma given off. Cold beer numbs the taste buds, making it impossible to distinguish the finer traits of a good beer.

On the other hand, serve those light beers very cold, because they don't have much taste to begin with.

BEER TASTING

One of the best ways to learn about beer is to have a beer tasting. Select one style of beer and have at least five different samples. This will enable you to taste the differences found in the same style of beer. Or select five different styles of beer. In this case you should serve the lightest beer first and gradually move on to the heavier.

Suggested 20-point beer evaluation system

Appearance (0 to 3 points)
Colors – These can range from light gold to black. They may described as pale, caramel, chocolate or gold. The type of malted barley used in the brewing produces the colors.

Aroma (0 to 4 points)
By simply smelling the ingredients in the glass, you can tell much about its makeup. A sweet aroma indicates the presence of malted barley. A flowery or bitter scent means the presence of hops. Usually brewers try to balance out these aromas, but sometimes one is meant to be stronger.

Taste (0 to 10 points)
Terms used to describe taste include fruity, nutty, flowery, hoppy, malty, sweet, bitter, grassy, crisp, refreshing.

Overall impression (0 to 3 points)
Personal preferences: Did you like the beer? Now is the time to discuss the beer's characteristics.

Total =

CHAPTER NINE

Brew your own beer

There are two ways that you can go about brewing your own beer:

- Brew it at home using your own equipment, ingredients and recipes.
- Go to a brew-on-premises (BOP) shop. Here you rent their equipment, buy their ingredients, use their recipes and get their advice.

There are a number of good reasons why you might want to brew beer yourself. For one, it's cheaper than buying the commercial stuff. The beer in Canada suffers one of the highest tax burdens of any country in the world. According to a study on tax policies, 53% of what Canadians pay for beer goes to the government compared to the world average of 32%.

Secondly, brewing you own lets you avoid the mass-marketed beer. When you brew your own, you are usually exposed to new products that open a whole new world of beer.

Finally there is self-satisfaction in making your own beer.

THE BREW-AT-HOME OR STOVE-TOP METHOD

There is certainly a unique status in brewing beer at home. You go out and get your own equipment (cost is about $150). You get a book of recipes and instructions and you brew your own beer, maybe just like your grandfather did.

But it could be similar to that exercise equipment that you bought, used once and put in the basement.

Basic homebrewing starter kit:

- Airlock – An inexpensive way to let carbon dioxide escape from the fermenter.
- Bottles – These should be reusable. Some homebrewers use glass bottles, but then you'll need a bottle capper as well. You can purchase refillable plastic bottles from your home brewing supplier.
- Bottle brush – For cleaning the bottles.
- Bottle washer – A curved tube that fits on your water faucet. It makes cleaning those bottles a lot easier.
- Bottling bucket and tube – Plastic (HDPE – high density polyethylene). These are cheap, simple devices that are necessary for the bottling stage.
- Brew pot – This must be stainless steel or enamel-coated. The pot should have at least a 16-quart capacity.
- Brewing spoon – This should be at least 18 inches long and be made of either stainless steel or plastic.
- Flexible plastic hose – This should be about 3 to 4 feet long.
- Primary fermentation vessel – A large (7 to 8 gallon) plastic bucket with a top and a hole for the airlock.
- Hydrometer – This device is necessary to determine the gravity of your brew. With this you are able to calculate the alcohol content.

All of the above can be purchased at any homebrewing supply shop. The supplier will also sell you a beer kit that contains all that you'll need to make the beer. These kits are sold by the beer style and most suppliers dispense lots of free advice.

THE BREW-ON-PREMISES (BOP) METHOD

The BOP shops opened as a protest to the high price of beer, which seems to be always going up. They began in British Columbia in the 1980s and the idea quickly spread to Ontario. There are now over 300 BOP shops, most of which are located in these provinces.

Initially there were more in Ontario but in 1993 the provincial government introduced a 26 cents per litre tax on the beer produced in these establishments. This came as result of a lobby from the large breweries, which felt their business was being affected. Many operations closed as a result of the loss of business and in 1994 the tax was lowered to 13 cents per litre.

How does a brew-on-premise operate?

Customers come in and select the ingredients for the brew they wish to make. This will come from a recipe usually supplied by the operator. Customers must then weigh out the ingredients and mix them in the kettle. Water is added and the mixture is cooked for a period of time producing the wort.

At the end of the brewing time, the wort is flash-cooled and poured into a carboy. Yeast is then added so that fermentation can occur. According to the law, the customer may be assisted with the process up to this point, but they must add the yeast themselves. The carboy is then moved into the primary fermentation room and left there for about a week. Over the course of the week the wort becomes beer. Some operations supply pre-made wort and the customer just comes in and adds the yeast.

The beer is then transferred to a cold room for aging. Here the beer is normally filtered and carbonated by the BOP operators. Clients come back to bottle their beer. They can purchase reusable bottles from the operator. Clients can even bring in their own keg, which is filled with their brew and taken home for use with their own tap system.

According to surveys, clients originally come in to make a copy of their own favorite brand, which is usually one of the mass-marketed lagers. But by their third visit they have seen others in the shop making less commercial beers and decide to give one a try. It might be an English bitter or a Czech lager but Canadians want to try something new. Gradually the BOP customers become more sophisticated and eventually move on to microbrew beers that they initially wouldn't touch.

Advantages of BOP shops

1. You don't have to buy all that equipment. They have very advanced and sophisticated apparatus.
2. If anything goes wrong with your brew (like it doesn't taste right) the BOP shop will often replace your batch.
3. Things are less likely to go wrong because the BOP equipment is ultra-clean and they know how to take care of it properly.
4. A greater variety of recipes are available.
5. The operators usually have an extensive background and knowledge of the brewing process.

CHAPTER TEN

Cooking and dining with beer

COOKING WITH BEER

Cuisine à la bière is rooted in Western Europe, in particular, Belgium, northern France, Germany and Great Britain. In Belgium and northern France, where beers that are totally unique in flavor are found, the chefs offer dishes to match these different tastes. Traditional dishes like Carbonnade Flamande are world famous. German food is heartier, such as sausages and sauerkraut cooked in wheat beer or Marzen. In Britain popular pub meals are often merged with traditional ales, porters and stouts.

As a liquid to cook with, beer is without rival. Milk does have its place when you are creating creamy sauces, but you wouldn't use it in a recipe for chili. Wine is used by many, but it doesn't have the versatility of beer. Water is very useful but lacks the additional flavors that beer can add to a dish.

Because of its tremendous variety of styles and tastes, beer is the ideal liquid to be used in cooking. Don't worry about the calories, as most of the alcohol is cooked off when you use beer in a beer recipe. Alcohol has a much lower boiling temperature than water, so it evaporates quickly when you heat up your dish, leaving the flavor of the beer.

Here are some suggested ways that you might use beer in your cooking:

- As a marinade for tenderizing or adding flavor to meats. Try soaking those cheaper cuts of meat in a mixture of English ale and spices for several hours. For a real gourmet treat, marinate a porterhouse steak with porter (you could substitute Guinness if no porter is available).

- As a cooking liquid. How about steaming Bavarian sausages in Oktoberfest beer?
- As a substitute for water in soups. Instead of water pour several cups of beer into the pot. Lighter soups are best with Pilsner-style beers, while stews get their best flavor when mixed with Scottish ale, porters or stouts.
- As a batter for fried foods. Light lagers or pale ales give a nice zing to the batter.
- As a cooking liquid for shellfish, like mussels or shrimp. Use a sweeter beer like lambic or a Trappist ale.
- As a cooking medium for roast chicken. Simply add a bottle of a Marzen or a porter and cook the leftover liquid to make a wonderful gravy.
- Also good in chili, baked beans, cheese dips and bread.
- As a dessert. Go ahead, be adventurous and mix a little stout with your chocolate ice cream.

When cooking with beer, be sure to keep the beer's primary flavor in mind. Malty beers add a sweet and nutty taste while hoppy lagers give the dishes a bitter or herbal flavor. Keep in mind that beer increases in bitterness as it reduces, so use a sweeter or malty beer when cooking for a long time. In addition, dark beers will add color to the food.

Dining with beer

There are several suggestions as to how to match food with different beer styles.

- Think ale for red wine and lager for white wine. Going back to your teachings of serving red wines with meat and white wines with fowl or fish, just substitute ale or lager appropriately. For example, serve a full-bodied brown ale with roast beef and a Pilsner with chicken.
- Select a beer from the same region as the meal. For example, dark Vienna lager goes well with spicy Mexican food; Marzen or Oktoberfest with German sausages; a British pale ale with steak or shepherd's pie; India's Kingfisher with a curry dish.

The following chart gives a list of various foods and the beer style that might go best with it:

Cuisine	Beer
Soups	
Light soups	Hoppy Pilsners, Pale ales
Heavy soups and stews	Scottish ales, Brown ales
Cheeses	
Soft cheeses	Lambic, stout, old ales
Cheddar	English bitter
Strong cheeses	porter, stout, bière en garde, Trappist ales, Rauchbier,
Salads	Wheat, Pilsner
Red meats	
Steak	Pale ales, porter
Hamburger	Pale lagers, Pale ales
Roast beef	India pale ale
Leg of lamb	Scottish ales, brown ales,
Game (venison, etc.)	Brown ales, porter
Chicken	Maibock, premium lager
Pork	Vienna lager, pale ale, wheat beer
Sausages	Marzen, Rauchbier, wheat beer
Seafood	
White fish	Pilsner
Salmon	Stout
Shellfish	Porter
Oysters	Dry stout (Guinness)
Spicy dishes	
Mexican, hot chili, Buffalo wings	Bock, Vienna dark lager, dark ales
Pizza	Light lagers or ales
Vegetable dishes	Pilsners, premium lagers
Creamy desserts	Bocks (double and triple), Russian stout
Fruity desserts	Fruit lambic, Witbier, porter, stout

- For an after-dinner treat, serve Barley wine, Eisbock, Trappist ales, double bock, triple bock.

CHAPTER ELEVEN

Beer as food

Beer: so much more than just a breakfast drink.
> – Seen on T-shirt

Since the earliest of times, beer has been considered a nutritious food. Even primitive man soon realized that when grain went through the beer-making process, the starchy insides of it were transformed into proteins and sugars that were not previously available.

By the Middle Ages water tended to be unsafe for drinking as nearly every water supply was polluted. Beer became a safe alternative to the tainted water. In the mid-1400s, Sir John Fortesque wrote of the English peasants: "They drink no water unless it is for devotion" (i.e., holy water).

All through the ages, beer was an important part of the everyday diet. Until the 1900s, children in both Europe and America were given weak beer, sometimes called small beer, regularly for breakfast and as a tonic for their health. Many Europeans have always referred to beer as "a bottle of liquid bread." In 1901 the British Parliament passed the Intoxicating Liquor Act, which forbade the sale of any intoxicating beverages, including beer, to children under the age of 14. Similar laws were passed in most of the Western world.

In the 1800s nursing mothers in Germany were encouraged to drink as many as seven pints of beer a day to aid in their breastfeeding. Many doctors prescribed beer as a tonic to patients who were thought of as weak and tired. In the 1500s a typical breakfast consisted of a loaf of bread, two quarts of beer and two pieces of salt fish. The children were only given one quart of beer each. Beer was, in fact, the breakfast drink.

GUINNESS IS GOOD FOR YOU

Guinness used an ad campaign "Guinness is good for you" for years. In the 1940s and 1950s, their ads contained testimonials from physicians who claimed that they had prescribed Guinness to their patients as a healthful tonic. Given current medical evidence, these doctors were not too far off the mark.

BEER AND HEALTH

Beer, if drank in moderation, softens the temper, cheers the spirit, and promotes health. —Thomas Jefferson

Is beer healthy?

Beer in moderation is a wholesome beverage that is made from natural ingredients.

Like anything else that is overused by the body, beer and other alcoholic drinks are dangerous when used in excess. But for most moderate drinkers, beer is very nutritious.

The average Canadian beer contains:
- 0 g of fat
- 0 mg cholesterol
- 25 mg sodium
- 13 g carbohydrate
- protein, calcium, potassium, phosphorus and vitamins B, B2 and B6

Calories and Alcohol in Canadian Beer

Regular beer	alcohol by volume 5%	• calories 150
Light beer	alcohol by volume 4%	• calories 110
Dry beer	alcohol by volume 5.5%	• calories 150
Premium malt liquor	alcohol by volume 6%	• calories 175
Ice beer	alcohol by volume 5.5%	• calories 150

Note: The alcohol is more than two-thirds of the caloric content.

SIX FACTS ABOUT BEER AND HEALTH

1. **Beer is fat-free and cholesterol-free.** The old idea that drinking beer will make you fat just isn't true. Beer isn't really that high in calories. Other popular beverages, like wine, juice soft drinks and milk, all contain more calories than beer. Beer does, however, stimulate the appetite when consumed in moderate quantities. This is sometimes considered to be an asset of alcohol but could be detrimental to health when people eat more than they should.

2. **Beer helps to improve blood circulation and helps to prevent heart disease.** Moderate amounts of alcohol help to increase the body's HDL cholesterol levels (that's the good cholesterol). This in turn helps to cut down on the incidence of deposits on the artery walls.

    Several years ago a report was published that stated that red wine was beneficial to a person's health. Recently, John Folks, the man who discovered that aspirin helps in the prevention of heart disease, brought out a report on the benefits of certain beers. He stated that dark beer contains substances called flavenoids, which are also found in red wine and tea. These flavenoids reduce the tendency of blood platelets to stick together (and thus clot) and activate plasminogen, a naturally produced substance, that aids in the breakup of blood clots. Several studies have concluded that moderate beer drinkers have a lower rate of fatal heart disease than non-beer drinkers.

3. **Beer is a nutritious drink.** Back in the Middle Ages people did not trust the drinking water. Instead they drank beer, which was boiled. They called beer "liquid bread" for good reason. Beer served not only as a thirst quencher but also as a necessary component of their diet.

4. **Beer helps you sleep better.** Moderate consumption of beer has a positive effect on sleep patterns because of the presence of the alcohol, hops (bittering substances) and phenols (aromas from the hops and grains).

5. **Beer and stress.** Due to its comparatively low alcohol content, beer has a relaxing effect on the body. A glass of beer

after work or before going to bed can have positive effects on an individual in terms of relieving stress.

6. **Beer and senior citizens.** Beer consumption in moderation has many positive effects on the elderly. It aids in blood vessel dilation, urination promotion and sleep. In the United States some nursing homes have "senior pub hours." As well as being healthy these beer-related innovations have improved sociability. Many European countries have adopted this practice. In Britain the benefits of grandfather going to the pub for a midday pint with his cronies have been known for a long time. There have also been suggestions that a regular beer may help retard aging.

These facts are not to suggest that you should go out and drink beer for medicinal reasons. Certainly improved diet, rest and exercise will go a lot further than tossing back a few pints. But it is important to know that beer drinking in moderation does not harm your health. Just remember the key phrase: in moderation.

CHAPTER TWELVE

The beer adventure

WHERE DO YOU GO TO FIND A GOOD BEER?

BREW PUBS

There are about 70 brew pubs operating in Canada and over 600 in the United States. Most are small and only put out a few different brands at one time but recently chains of brew pubs have started to appear both in Canada and in the U.S. Going to brew pubs is a great way to learn about and sample new and different beers.

Here are some of the good reasons for visiting brew pubs:

- **Serving knowledge** In a brew pub they know how to serve a particular style of beer. They will serve it at the proper temperature and in the proper glass. (You won't get a frosted mug in these places.)
- **Background knowledge** The servers (quite often the owners) know about the beers that the pub is serving. They are usually quite willing to give you tastes of their products and are very capable of explaining the nuances of each beer being served.
- **Friendly and co-operative** Most brew pub employees are anxious to sell their product. They can usually tell you about the brewing process and their equipment. You might even be offered a short tour of the facilities.
- **Fresh beer** Beer in a brew pub is about as fresh as you can get. In the U.K. they call the pub located beside a brewery a "beer tap" because the beer is so fresh. The beer only travels from the back room of the brewery to the tap in front of you, instead of being transported over long distances.

- **Variety** Most brew pubs offer several different styles of beer. They will usually have a flagship brew, their best seller or best brew. But they will also have several others for you to try. Sometimes the pub will have an imported beer, just so you can compare. Really good brew pubs will have a regular "guest beer" from one of the other breweries – kind of a co-op beer program.
- **Special programs** Some brew pubs have the occasional guest speaker come in to share some of his knowledge and experience with the regulars.
- **Good food** Most brew pubs know the value of serving good food at their establishments. Often they will present a menu with items cooked with their beer. The servers should be able to suggest proper food and beer matches.

Here is a list of some very good brew pubs across the nation.

- The Granite Brewery, 122 Barrington St., Halifax, NS
- The Granite Brewery, 245 Eglinton Ave East, Toronto, ON (sister brew pub to the original one in Halifax)
- The Kingston Brewing Company, 34 Clarence St., Kingston, ON
- Spinnakers Brewing, 308 Catherine St., Victoria, BC
- Brewsters Brewing Company and Restaurant, brew pub chain located in Calgary, Edmonton, Lethbridge, Regina and Moosejaw
- Le Cheval Blanc, 809 rue Ontario, Montreal, PQ
- Swan's Brew Pub, 506 Pandora St., Victoria, BC
- Steamworks Brewing Company, 375 Water St., Vancouver, BC
- Amsterdam Brewing Company, 600 King St. W., Toronto, ON
- The Olde Stone Brew Pub, 380 George St. N., Peterborough, ON

A complete list of all the current brew pubs in Canada is in Appendix 2.

OTHER GOOD PUBS

If a pub can't be a brew pub, then it should still try to offer a good selection of beers. It is not uncommon for a good pub to have as many as 30 different draft beers on tap. Draft beer is superior to bottled because it is unpasteurized, fresher and has a better taste.

Occasionally you'll find a pub that specializes in bottled beers of the world. Some will have hundreds of different beers. While these can be quite pricey, this might be the only opportunity you'll ever have to sample some the more exotic beers from around the world.

BREWERY TOURS

Most breweries offer tours and there is usually a tasting afterwards. But instead of going to one of the big, mass-producing breweries, go and visit a microbrewery. Most of them have tours on selected days and the beer afterwards is a lot better.

There is a complete list of the microbreweries in Canada at the back in Appendix 1. Give them a call and go on tour.

The Ale Trail

From April through October on seven different weekends you can visit six different craft breweries in Southern Ontario. On the trail you get an opportunity to meet the brew masters, tour the brew houses, see demonstrations and sample the beers, all for free. You are welcome to visit these breweries anytime, but on the Ale Trail you get to experience special events and unique beer sampling.

The six breweries involved in the Ale Trail are:

- Brick Brewing Company, 181 King St. S., Waterloo, ON
- Gold Crown Brewery, 71 King St., N., Waterloo, ON
- Old Mill Brewery, 55 Mill St., W., Elora, ON
- Wellington County Brewery, 950 Woodlawn Rd. W., Guelph, ON
- F&M Brewery, 355 Elmira Rd., N., Guelph, ON
- Sleeman Brewing and Malting, 551 Clair Rd. W., Guelph, ON

You can start your tour at any one of the breweries. For more information contact Ale Trail, P.O. Box 210226, Campus Postal Outlet, 35 Harvard Rd.,Guelph, ON N1G 4T3, <www.AleTrail.on.ca>.

BEER FESTIVALS

By far the best way to explore the world of beer tasting is to go to a beer festival. Here you'll have a wealth of microbreweries set up. This type of event is usually held outdoors with the brewery displays under huge tents, each in their own little booth. All of the brewery reps will be anxious to talk up their beers and to give you samples.

Normally you pay a healthy entrance fee but you get a lot of freebies to balance the cost. On entrance you'll receive a set number of tokens that can be exchanged for small samples at the various booths. If you run out of tokens you can purchase more for a nominal fee. You will be given a souvenir sampling glass and a program. The samples are generally of the two to three ounce variety, but that's okay, because then you can sample a greater variety of beers.

Since these are called festivals, there is usually a lot more going on than just the beer tasting (although that is the main point of the exercise). Most have musical entertainment and some have guest speakers and demonstrations.

Some suggestions

1. Go early and try to avoid the big rush. Some of these events are very popular and attract huge crowds.
2. Use the festival program. It's organized to show where to go in an orderly fashion. Follow it and you won't miss any of the booths.
3. Clean out your glass between tastings. This is essential because most of the craft brews will coat the inside of the glass, leaving residue that will taint your next tasting. There should be water taps or rinsers available so that you can clean out your glass between tastings.
4. Eat! Don't try tasting beer on an empty stomach. Most festivals will have a variety of good food on hand, sometimes offered by the local pubs who might have set up their own booths. Avoid eating spicy or greasy foods. These types of food will seriously affect your tastebuds. If you are bringing your own food, things like bread, pretzels and crackers are a good way to cleanse the palate.

5. Take notes. The serious beer taster will bring a notepad and pencil. You'll be surprised what you forget if you don't write it down as you wander around consuming beers.

6. Don't try to taste every beer in the festival. In most cases this is impossible. Have a tasting plan and try to carry it out. In addition there is no sense in heading for your favorite brews. You've already tasted these! Go on out and try something new. Be adventurous.

8. Don't drink and drive. Use a DD (designated driver), call a cab or use the public transportation system.

A few Canadian beer festivals

- Great Canadian Brewery Festival, University of Guelph, mid-September
- Great Canadian Beer Festival, Victoria, BC, early November
- Toronto Festival of Beer, Fort York, Toronto, ON, early August
- East Coast Festival of Beer, Halifax, NS, September
- Festibière de Chambly, Chambly, PQ, early September
- Great British British Beer Festival, London, England, early August
- Great American Beer Festival, Denver, Colorado, early October

Now go out and be adventurous and try a new beer. There are thousands of great brews just waiting for you to taste.

Microbreweries in Canada

BRITISH COLUMBIA

Bear Brewing Company, 965 McGill Place, Kamloops, BC.
Established 1994. *Brands*: Black Bear Ale, Brown Bear Ale, Polar
Bear Lager.

Beaver Beer Brewing Company, 703-1399 Fountain Way,
Vancouver, BC. Established 1998.
Brands: Beaver Tale Ale Blonde Beaver Ale.

Bowen Island Brewing Company, 3300 Bridgeway St. Vancouver,
BC. Established 1994. *Brands*: Blonde, Bowen Ale, Bowen
Special Bitter, Hemp Cream Ale.

Copper Kettle Brewing Ltd., 26004 Fraser Highway, Aldergrove,
BC. Established 1998. *Brands*: Nut Brown Ale, Stinger Ale,
Timber Wolf Pale Ale.

Coquihalla Brewery, 1679 Cliveden Ave., Delta, BC.
Established 1997. *Brands*: Brother Lager, Premium Lager.

Gulf Island Brewing Company, 270 Furness Rd., Salt Spring
Island, BC. Established 1997. *Brands*: Bureaucracy Bitter,
Pender Island Porter, Salt Spring Golden Ale.

Horseshoe Bay Brewery, 1481 Dominion St., North Vancouver, BC,
(moved from Horseshoe Bay to North Vancouver).
Established 1982 (one of Canada's earliest microbreweries)
Brands: Bay Ale, Christmas Ale, IPA, Nut Brown Ale, Pale Ale,
Strange Brew, Triple Frambozen,

Hagar's Brewing Company, 235 W. 1st St., North Vancouver, BC.
Brands: Grizzly Nut Brown Ale, Hagar's Honey Pilsner,
Lohin's ESB, Narwhal Pale Ale, Scandinavian Lager.

Lighthouse Brewing Company, 2-836 Devonshire Rd., Victoria, BC. Established 1998. *Brands*: Race Rocks Ale.

Nelson Brewing Company, 512 Latimer St. Nelson, BC. Established 1900. *Brands*: Blackheart, Nelson After Dark, Old Brewery Ale, Paddywhack India Pale Ale, Silverking Premium Lager, Valhalla Gold.

R&B Brewing Company, 54 E. 4th Ave., Vancouver, BC, Established 1997. *Brands*: R&B's Raven Ale, Red Devil Ale.

Russell Brewing, 202-13018 80th Ave., Surrey, BC. Established 1995. *Brands*: Russell Cream Ale, Russell Amber Ale, Christmas Ale.

Shaftebury Brewing,, (now owned by Sleeman's), 7989 82nd St., Delta, BC. *Brands*: Cream Ale, Rainforest Amber Ale, Honey Pale Ale, Hefeweizen Wheat Ale, Paul And Tim's Original West Coast Winter Ale.

Storm Brewing Ltd., 310 Commercial Dr., Vancouver, BC. Established 1995. *Brands*: Black Berry Lambic, Black Cherry Lambic, Espresso Ale, Ginger Beer, Hurricane India Pale Ale, Midnight Porter, Raspberry Lambic, Highland Scottish Ale.

Tall Ship Ale Co., 39002-E Discovery Way, Squamish, BC. *Brands*: No. 1 Barley Wine, IPA, Raspberry Cream Ale, Black Ship, Smoked Porter, Tall Ship Ale, Imperial Stout.

Tin Whistle Brewing Company, 954 W. Eckhardt Ave., Penticton, BC. Established 1995. *Brands*: Penticton Pale Ale, Rattlesnake ESB, Black Widow Dark Ale, Coyote Ale, Peaches'n Cream, Killer Bee Honey Ale.

Tree Brewing Company, 1083 Richter St., Kelowna, BC. Established 1995. *Brands*: Amber Ale, Spy Dark Lager, Lager, Tree Red Ale, Tree Pale Ale, Spiced Midwinter Ale.

Vancouver Island Brewing, 2330 Government St., Victoria, BC. Established 1985. *Brands*: Piper's Pale Ale, Hermann's Dark Lager, Victoria Lager, Blonde Ale, Victoria Weizen, Hermannator Ice Bock.

Whistler Brewing Company, 1209 Alpha Lake Rd., Whistler, BC. Established 1989. *Brands*: Black Tusk Ale, Whistler Pale Ale, Whistler Premium Lager, Whistler's Mother Pale Ale, Whistler Cream Ale.

Wild Horse Brewing Company, 399 Main St., Penticton, BC.
  Brands: Brown Ale, Blonde Ale, Pale Ale, Dark Ale.
Windermere Valley Brewing Ltd., Invermere, BC.
  Established 1998. *Brands*: Copper, Gold.

ALBERTA

Alley Kat Brewing Company, 9929 60th Ave., Edmonton, AB,
  Established 1994. *Brands*: Alley Kat Amber, Full Moon,
  Aprikat, Scona Gold.
Banff Brewing, 5815 29 St. NE, Calgary, AB.
  Brands: Dancing Bear Pale Ale, Storm Mountain Bavarian Dark,
  Cutthroat Amber.
Bow Valley Brewing Company, 109 Boulder Cres., Canmore, AB.
  Established 1995. *Brands*: Premium Lager, Bruno's Mountain
  Bock, Saddleback Pils.
Brew Brothers Brewing Company, 6025 Centre St. S., Calgary,
  AB. Established 1994. *Brands*: Black Pilsner, Alberta Gold
  Bock, Ambush Ale, Prairie Steam, Dopplebock, Pale Ale.
Flanagan & Sons Brewing Company, 7921 Coronet Rd.,
  Edmonton, AB. *Brands*: Bitter and Twisted, Pale Tommy,
  Wheathead.
Wild Rose Brewery Ltd., 40th St. SE, Calgary, AB. Established 1996.
  Brands: Wild Nut Brown Ale, Goosebump Pale Ale, Oktoberfest
  Wheat Ale, Wheat Red Ale.

MANITOBA

Fort Garry Brewing Company, 1249 Clarence Ave., Winnipeg, MB.
  Brands: Fort Garry Ale, Fort Garry Dark Lager, Fort Garry Pale
  Ale.
The Folks Market Brewing Company, Winnipeg, MB.
Two Rivers Brewing Company, 551 Ferry St., Winnipeg, MB,

ONTARIO

Ambassador Brewing Company, 4045 Seminole St., Windsor, ON,
  Brands: Irish Red Beer, Oatmeal Stout, Shoreline Lager.
Amber Brewing Company, 1095 Strathy, Unit 8, Mississauga, ON.

Amsterdam Brewing Company, 600 King St. W., Toronto, ON. *Brands*: Natural Blonde, Nut Brown Ale, Natural Light, Dutch Amber, Kerstmis Bier, Framboise, Highland Red, Oktoberfest, Scotch Ale, Spring Bock, Wheat Beer.

Cameron's Brewing Company, 1 Westside Dr., Unit 4, Toronto, ON, Established 1997. *Brands*: Cameron's Auburn Ale, Cameron's Cream Ale.

Cool Beer Brewing Company, 54 Bramsteele Rd., Unit 20, Brampton, ON, Established 1997.

Creemore Springs Brewery, 139 Mill St., Creemore, ON, Established 1987. *Brands*: Creemore Springs Premium Lager, Ur Bock (Seasonal).

Durham Brewing Company, 1885 Clements Rd., Pickering, ON, Established 1996. *Brands*: Black Katt, Durham ESB, Durham Triple X.

F&M Brewery, 355 Elmira Rd. (Melran Mall), Guelph, ON. *Brands*: MacLeans Pale Ale, Stone Hammer Pilsner, Eramosa Honey Wheat, Royal City Cream Ale, F&M Special Draft, Royal City Lager.

Gold Crown Brewery, 71 King St. N., Waterloo, ON. (next to the Huether Hotel), Established 1995. *Brands*: Kings Pilsener, Jesters Ale, Poets Warrior Lager, Friars Traditional Dark.

Great Lakes Brewing Company, 30 Queen Elizabeth Blvd., Etobicoke, ON. Established 1987. *Brands*: Great Lake lager, Red Leaf Lager.

Hart Brewing Company Ltd., 175 Industrial Ave., Carlton Place, ON, Established 1991. *Brands*: Amber Ale, Cream Ale, Festive Brown Ale, Finnigans Irish Red Ale, Mississippi Steamboat, Mississippi Timbertown, Valley Gold, Hardy Stout, Honey Wheat, Maple Brown Ale. Contract Brews: Dragons Breath Pale Ale, Banks, Scotch Irish Session Ale.

Hogtown Brewing Company, 2351 Royal Windsor Dr., Mississauga, ON, Established 1994. *Brands*: Gold Draft

Kawartha Lakes Brewing Company, 687 Rye St., Peterborough, ON, Established 1996. *Brands*: Cream Ale, Pale Ale, Nut Brown Ale, Raspberry Wheat.

Lakes of Muskoka Cottage Brewery, 13 Taylor Rd.,
Bracebridge, ON, Established 1996.
Brands: Muskoka Cream Ale, Muskoka Steam Beer

Magnotta Brewery, 271 Chrislea Rd., Vaughan, ON, and 1760
Midland Ave., Scarborough, ON. Established 1996.
Brands: Magnotta Traditional Altbier, True North Premium
Cream Ale, True North, Premium Lager, True North Premium
Light, True North Premium Strong Ale.

Neustadt Springs Brewery Ltd., 456 Jacob St., Neustadt, ON.
Brands: Belgium Lager, Scotch Heavy Ale.

Niagara Falls Brewing Company, 6863 Lundy's Lane, Niagara
Falls, ON. *Brands*: Eisbock, Limited Edition, Gritstone Ale,
Cherry Kriek, Maple Wheat, Brock Extra Stout, Olde Jack Bitter
Strong Ale, Saaz Pilsner, Niagara Trapper Cold Filtered Draft,
Apple Ale.

Old Credit Brewing Company, 6 Queen St. W., Port Credit, ON.
Brands: Amber Ale, Pale Pilsner

The Old Mill Brewery, 55 Mill St. W., Elora, ON (on the site of the
old Taylor & Bates Brewery). Established 1997. *Brands*: Irish
Ale, Rye, ESB, Grand Ale, Paddy's Irish Red.

Quinte Brewery, 150 Sydney St., Belleville, ON. *Brands*: Antler
Draft, Loyalist Lager, Quinte Gold, Reel Lager, Sir John 'Eh'.

Robinson Brewing, 2390 Cawthra Rd., Mississauga, ON. *Brands*:
Cream Ale, Cream Lager, Dark, Light, Pilsner, Red, Super Dry.

Scotch Irish Brewing Company Inc., 4197 Limestone Rd.,
Kinborn, ON, Established 1998. *Brands*: Scotch Irish Session
Ale (contract brewed by Hart Brewing).

Taylor & Bate, 75 Paul St., St. Catharines, ON (formerly located in
Elora). Established 1998. *Brands*: Niagara Spray Premium
Lager and some seasonal beers.

Trafalgar Brewing Company, Oakville, ON. *Brands*: Harbour
Gold, Potside Amber, Abbey Belgian, Downrigger Bock, Granery
Wheat, Red Hill Mild.

Walkerville Brewing Company, 525 Argyle Rd., Walkerville, ON,
Established 1998. *Brands*: Walkerville Lager.

Wellington County Brewery, 950 Woodlawn Rd. W., Guelph, ON. Established 1984. One of the earliest microbreweries in Ontario. Wellington has remained a cottage brewery and was the first North American brewery in modern times to brew cask-conditioned "Real Ale." One of six breweries found on the Ale Trail. *Brands*: County Ale, Arkell Best Bitter, Iron Duke, Honey Lager, Premium Lager, Special Pale Ale.

Woodbridge Brewing Company, 300 Trowers Rd., Woodbridge, ON, Established 1996.
Brands: Arctic Gold, Europa Lager, White.

QUEBEC

Brasserie Aux 4 Temps, 480 Martineau Ouest, St-Hyancinthe, PQ. Established 1996. *Brands*: Gargouille Blonde, Gargouille Rousse, L'Exaltee, La Chope, La Monteregienne, Stouque

Brasserie Le Chaudron, 5710 Garnier, Montreal, PQ. Established 1998. *Brands*: Coeur d'or.

Brasserie McAuslan, 4850 St. Ambroise, Montreal, PQ.
Brands: St. Ambroise Oatmeal Stout, St. Ambroise Pale Ale, Griffon Brown Ale, Griffon Extra Pale Ale, McAuslan Cream Ale, McAuslan Strong Ale, Angus, Frontenac.

Broue Chope, 46 Industriel, St-Eustache, PQ. *Brands*: La Chimere.

Ferme Brasserie Schoune (Farm Brewery), 295 rue Industrielle, St-Odilon, PQ. Established 1997.
Brands: La Beauceronne, La Beauceronne a l'erable, Schoune Ambree, Schoune Beige, Schoune Blonde ,Schoune Forte

La Barberie, 310, rue St-Roch, Quebec City, PQ. Established 1997.
Brands: Amber Ale, Stout, Weizen (all draft on contract).

La Brasserie Seigneuriale, (now owned by Sleeman's), 135-D Chemin du Tremblay, Boucherville, PQ. *Brands*: La Seigneuriale, La Seigneuriale Blonde, La Seigneuriale Reserve, La Seigneuriale Triple.

Les Bieres de Nouvelle-France, Saint-Paulin, PQ, Established 1998.
Brands: Ambree de Sarrasin, Blonde d'epeautre, Claire Fontaine.

Les Brasseurs GMT, 5585 rue de la Roche, Montreal, PQ. *Brands*: Belle Gueule, Belle Gueule Rousse, Canon, Blanche de L'ile, Mona Lisa.

Les Brasseurs de l'Anse, 182 route 170, Anse Saint-Jean, PQ.
Established 1997. *Brands*: Angus, Illegale, Illegale Dry, La Folie
Douce, La Royalle.

Les Brasseurs du Nord, 875 Michele-Bohec, Blainville, PQ.
Established 1987. *Brands*: Boreale-Blonde, Cuivree, Doree,
Noire, Rousse.

Lion D'or (Golden Lion Brewing), 6 College St., Lennoxville, PQ.
Brands: Bishop's Blonde, Lion's Pride, Tailgater Amber Ale Black
Fly Stout, Townships' Pale Ale

Micro-Brasserie Charlevoix, 37 rue Saint-Jean Baptiste,
Baie Saint-Paul, PQ. Established 1998.
Brands: Ambree Blonde, Brune, Octoberfest, Rousse.

Microbrasserie Saint-Arnold, 435 rue Paquette, Saint-Jovite, PQ
Brands: Bierede l'Eveque, Bieredes Anges, La Vlimeuse,
Minereva, Minerva Dry, Muchacha.

NEW BRUNSWICK

Picaroons, 349 King St., Fredericton, NB. Established 1995.
Brands: Crooked Log Blonde Ale, Irish Red Ale, Pipers Best
Bitter, Timber Hog Stout, Whale Ale, Autumn Harvest Ale,
Horny Toad Ale, Old Red Nose Christmas Ale, Picaroons Winter
Warmer, Scotch Ale, Summer Witbeer, Thunderhead Extra
Special Bitter.

NOVA SCOTIA

Garrison Brewing Company, 6300 Lady Hammond Rd., Halifax,
NS, Established 1997. *Brands*: Garrison Barrack Street Brown,
Garrison McNabs Special, Garrison Red Ale, Jalapeno Ale,

Maritime Beer Company, 62 Windmill Drive, Halifax, NS.
Brands: Privateer's Pale Ale, Halifax 1749, Black Pearl Cream
Ale, King's Honey Amber, Atlantic Storm.

The New Scotland Brewing Company, 102 Front St., Pictou, NS.
Brands: Scotsman Golden Rye Ale, Scotsman Wheat Ale.

Propeller Brewing Company, 2015 Gottingen St., Halifax, NS,
Established 1997. *Brands*: Pale Ale, ESB, Tattoo Ale.

APPENDIX TWO

Canadian brew pubs

BRITISH COLUMBIA

Barley Mill,
Penticton, BC

Big River Brewing,
180-14200 Entertainment Way,
Richmond, BC

Buffalo Brew Pub,
Prince George, BC

Canoe Club/Knucklehead Brewing,
Heritage Quay, Victoria, BC

Howe Sound Inn and Brewery,
37801 Cleveland Ave., Squamish, BC

Mission Springs Brewing,
7160 Oliveer St., Mission, BC

Ridge Brewing,
Hwy. 3 & Hwy. 97, Osoyoos, BC

Sailor Hagar's Brew Pub,
221 W. 1st St., North Vancouver, BC

Spinnakers Brewing,
308 Catherine St., Victoria, BC

Steamworks Brewing Company,
375 Water St., Vancouver, BC

Swan's Pub/Buckerfield Brewery,
506 Pandora St., Victoria, BC

The Creek Brewery and Restaurant,
1253 Johnson St., Vancouver, BC

Yaletown Brewing,
1111 Mainland St., Vancouver, BC

ALBERTA

Brewsters Brewing Company and Restaurant,
834 11th Ave. SW, Calgary, AB

Brewsters Brewing Company and Restaurant,
176 755 Lake Bonavista Dr. SE,
Calgary, AB

Brewsters Brewing Company and Restaurant,
11620-104 Avenue, Edmonton, AB

Brewsters Brewing Company and Restaurant,
1814 Mayor Magrath Dr. S.,
Lethbridge, AB

Grizzly Paw Pub & Brewing Company,
622-8th St., Canmore, AB

Wild Trail Brewing Company and Taps,
Calgary Trail South, Edmonton, AB

Wildwood Pub and Grill,
2417 4th St. SW., Calgary, AB

SASKATCHEWAN

Barley Mill Brewing Company,
6155 Rochdale Blvd., Regina, SK

Bonzinni's Brew Pub,
4634 Albert St. S., Regina, SK

Brewsters Brewing Company and Restaurant,
1832 Victoria Ave. E., Regina, SK

Brewsters Brewing Company and Restaurant,
8 Main St. N., Moose Jaw, SK

Brewsters Brewing Company and Restaurant,
480 McCarthy Blvd. N., Regina, SK

Buffalo Brew Pub,
Chinook Center, 240 Central Ave.,
Swift Currant, SK

Clarks Crossing,
3030 Diefenbaker Dr., Saskatoon, SK

Fox and Hounds Brew Pub,
7 Assiniboine Dr., Saskatoon, SK

Hose and Hydrant Brewing Company,
612 11th St. E., Saskatoon, SK

Last Straw,
127 North Albert St., Regina, SK

McQuire's Irish Pub and Brewery,
2105 8th St. E., Grosvenor Park
Centre, Regina, SK

MANITOBA

Agassiz Brewing Company,
24 Terracon Pl., Winnipeg, MB

River City Brewing Company,
437 Stradbrook Ave., Osbourne
Village, Winnipeg, MB

The Pumphouse Brewing Company,
109 James Ave., Winnipeg, MB

ONTARIO

Al Frisco's,
133 John St., Toronto, ON

Brewer's Pub,
Smiths Falls, ON

C'est What?,
67 Front St. E., Toronto, ON

CEEPS Barney's Ltd.,
671 Richmond St., London, ON

Cellar Tap,
320 Bay St., Sault Ste. Marie, ON

Charley's Tavern,
4714 Tecumseh Rd. E., Windsor, ON

Clocktower Brew Pub,
575 Bank St., Ottawa, ON

Denison's Brewing Company,
75 Victoria St., Toronto, ON

Feathers,
962 Kingston Rd., Toronto, ON

Granite Brewery,
245 Eglinton Ave. East, Toronto, ON,

Kingston Brewing Company,
34 Clarence St., Kingston, ON

Lion Brewery
(in the Huether Hotel),
59 King St N., Waterloo, ON

Master's Brasserie and Brew Pub,
330 Queen St., Ottawa, ON

**Olde Heidelberg Brewery and
Restaurant**,
2 King St., Heidelberg, ON

Olde Stone Brew Pub,
380 George St. N.,
Peterborough, ON

Pepperwood Bistro,
1455 Lakeshore Rd., Burlington, ON

**Port Arthur Brasserie and Brew
Pub**,
901 Red River Rd., Thunder Bay, ON

**Tapster's Brewhouse and
Restaurant**,
100 Britannia Rd. E.,
Mississauga, ON

The Merchant Ale House
(Murray St. Brewing Company),
98 St. Paul St., St. Catharines, ON

Tin House Brew Pub,
453 Sussex Dr., Ottawa, ON

Tracks Brew Pub,
60 Queen St., Brampton, ON

QUEBEC

Brutopia,
1219 rue Crescent, Montréal, PQ

Chez Gambrinus,
3160 Boulevarde des Forges,
Trois-Rivières, PQ

Dieu du Ciel,
29 Laurier O., Montréal, PQ

L'Inox,
37 rue St-Andre, Quebec City, PQ

La Cervoise,
4457 St-Laurant, Montréal, PQ

La Diable,
3005 Chemin Principal, Mont
Tremblant, PQ

Microbrasserie Breughel,
68 Route 132, St-German de
Kamouraska, PQ

La Lambic du Nord 1,
Chemin de la Minerve,
La Minerve, PQ

La Microbrasserie St-Arnold,
435 rue Paquet, St-Jovite, PQ

La Taverne du Sergent Recreteur,
4650 St-Laurent Blvd., Montréal, PQ

Le Bilboquet,
1850 Rue des Cascades,
St-Hyacinthe, PQ

Le Cheval Blanc,
809 rue Ontario E., Montréal, PQ

Les Bières de Nouvelle-France Inc.,
Saint-Paulin, PQ

Vessels and Barrels,
220a Chemin du Lac Millette,
Carrefour des Trois Villages,
St-Sauveur-des-Monts, PQ

Vessels and Barrels,
6321 Route Transcanadienne,
Pointe Claire, PQ

NEW BRUNSWICK

Tapps Brew Pub and Steakhouse, 78
King St., Saint John, NB

NOVA SCOTIA

Granite Brewery, 1222 Barrington St.,
Halifax, NS

Paddy's Pub and Brewery, 42
Aberdeen St., Kentville, NS

The Queen Molly, 96 Water St.,
Yarmouth, NS

Rogue's Roost Ale House,
Spring Garden Rd. and Queen St.,
Halifax, NS

PRINCE EDWARD ISLAND

Lone Star Café and Brewery,
449 University Ave.,
Charlottetown, PEI

Ale family of beers

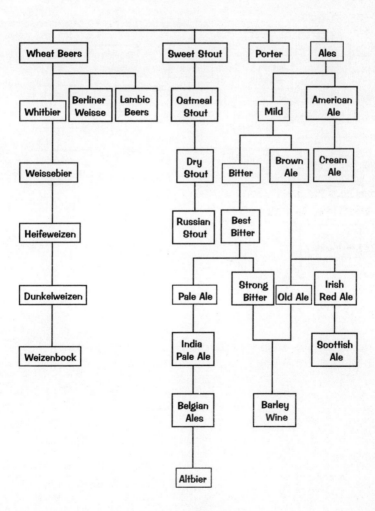

Lager family of beers

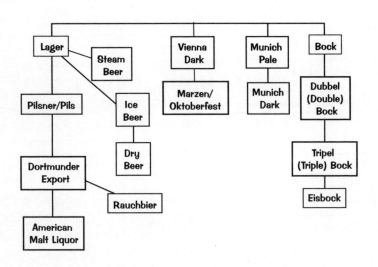

APPENDIX FIVE

Further reading and web sites

BOOKS

Brew pub Cookbook,
  by Stephen Beaumont, MacMillan Canada, 1997.

The Great Canadian Beer Book,
  by Stephen Beaumont, MacMillan Canada, 1993.

Michael Jackson's Beer Companion,
  by Michael Jackson, Philadelphia Running Press, 1993.

The New World Guide To Beer,
  by Michael Jackson, Philadelphia, Running Press, 1988.

Beer Lover's Companion,
  by Josh Leventhal, New York Black Dog and Leventhal, 1999.

Encyclopedia of Beer,
  by Christine Rhodes et al., New York Henry Holt, 1997.

Beer Enthusiasts Guide,
  by Gregg Smith, Bookcrafters, U.S.A., 1994.

Campaign for Real Ale (CAMRA): Good Beer Guide,
  by Neil Hansen (ed.), published annually by CAMRA.

The Good Pub Guide,
  by Alistair Aird (ed.), published annually by Vermillion Press.

Eric's Beer & Homebrewing Page
www. pekkel.uthsca.edu/beer

The Real Beer Page
www.realbeer.com

Beer Manifesto
www.netcom.ca/~jdoakes

Beer World
www.dailyglobe.com/beer

Canadian Beer Guide
www.canbeer.com

Anheuser-Busch Breweries
www.anheuser-busch.com

Coors Brewing
www.coorsandco.com

The Granite Brewery (Halifax and Toronto)
www.interlog.com/~granite

The Kingston Brewing Company
www.kingstonbrewing.com

Labatt Brewing
www.labatt.com

McAuslanBrewing, Montréal
vwww.mcauslan.com

Miller Brewing, Milwaukee
www.millerbrewing.com

Molson Brewing
www.molson.com

Wellington Waterloo Ale Trail
www.aletrail.on.ca

Unibroue, Chambly, PQ
www.unibroue.com

OVER 100 CLASSIC COLES NOTES ARE ALSO AVAILABLE:

SHAKESPEARE

- Antony and Cleopatra
- Antony and Cleopatra
  Questions & Answers
- As You Like it
- Hamlet
- Hamlet in Everyday English
- Hamlet – Questions & Answers
- Julius Caesar
- Julius Caesar in Everyday English
- Julius Caesar
  Questions & Answers
- King Henry IV – Part 1
- King Henry V
- King Lear
- King Lear in Everyday English
- King Lear – Questions & Answers
- Macbeth
- Macbeth in Everyday English
- Macbeth – Questions & Answers
- Measure for Measure
- Merchant of Venice
- Merchant of Venice
  in Everyday English
- Midsummer Night's Dream
- Midsummer Night's Dream
  Questions & Answers
- Much Ado About Nothing
- Othello
- Othello – Questions & Answers
- Richard II
- Richard III
- Romeo and Juliet
- Romeo and Juliet
  in Everyday English
- Romeo and Juliet
  Questions & Answers
- Taming of the Shrew
- Tempest
- Twelfth Night

SHAKESPEARE TSE*

- Hamlet T.S.E.
- Julius Caesar T.S.E.
- King Henry IV – Part I T.S.E.
- King Lear T.S.E.
- Macbeth T.S.E.
- Merchant of Venice T.S.E.
- Othello T.S.E.
- Romeo and Juliet T.S.E.
- Taming of the Shrew T.S.E.
- Tempest T.S.E.
- Twelfth Night T.S.E.
  •Total Study Edition

LITERATURE AND POETRY

- Animal Farm
- Brave New World
- Catch 22
- Catcher in the Rye, Nine Stories
- Chrysalids, Day of the Triffids
- Crucible
- Death of a Salesman
- Diviners
- Duddy Kravitz and Other Works
- Edible Woman
- Emma
- Fahrenheit 451
- Farewell to Arms
- Fifth Business
- Glass Menagerie
- Grapes of Wrath
- Great Expectations
- Great Gatsby
- Gulliver's Travels
- Heart of Darkness
- Huckleberry Finn
- Iliad
- Jane Eyre
- King Oedipus, Oedipus at Colonus
- Lord of the Flies
- Lord of the Rings, Hobbit
- Man for All Seasons
- Mayor of Casterbridge
- 1984
- Odyssey
- Of Mice and Men
- Old Man and the Sea
- One Flew Over the Cuckoos Nest
- Paradise Lost
- Pride and Prejudice
- Machiavelli's The Prince
- Scarlet Letter
- Separate Peace
- Stone Angel and Other Works
- Street Car Named Desire
- Surfacing
- Tale of Two Cities
- Tess of the D'Urbervilles
- To Kill a Mockingbird
- Two Solitudes
- Who Has Seen the Wind
- Wuthering Heights

THE CANTERBURY TALES

- The Canterbury Tales
- Prologue to the Canterbury Tales
  Total Study Edition
- Prologue to the Canterbury Tales
- French Verbs Simplified

HOW TO GET AN A IN ...

- Calculus
- Permutations, Combinations &
  Probability
- School Projects & Presentations
- Senior Algebra
- Senior English Essays
- Senior Physics
- Sequences & Series
- Statistics & Data Analysis
- Trigonometry & Circle Geometry

BIOLOGY

- Biology Notes

CHEMISTRY

- Elementary Chemistry Notes Rev.
- How to Solve Chemistry Problems
- Introduction to Chemistry

MATHEMATICS

- Elementary Algebra Notes
- Secondary School Mathematics 1
- Secondary School Mathematics 4

PHYSICS

- Elementary Physics Notes
- Senior Physics

REFERENCE

- Dictionary of Literary Terms
- Effective Term Papers and Reports
- English Grammar Simplified
- Handbook of English Grammar &
  Composition
- How to Write Good Essays & Critical
  Reviews
- Secrets of Studying English

**For fifty years, Coles Notes have been helping
students get through high school and university.
New Coles Notes will help get you through the rest of life.**

Look for these NEW COLES NOTES!

BUSINESS

- Effective Business Presentations
- Accounting for Small Business
- Write Effective Business Letters
- Write a Great Résumé
- Do a Great Job Interview
- Start Your Own Small Business
- Get Ahead at Work

GARDENING

- Indoor Gardening
- Perennial Gardening
- Herb Gardening
- Organic Gardening

LIFESTYLE

- Wine
- Bartending
- Beer
- Wedding
- Opera
- Casino Gambling
- Better Bridge
- Better Chess
- Better Tennis
- Better Golf
- Public Speaking
- Speed Reading
- Cooking 101
- Scholarships and Bursaries
- Cats and Cat Care
- Dogs and Dog Care

PARENTING

- Your Child: The First Year
- Your Child: The Terrific Twos
- Your Child: Ages Three and Four
- Raising A Reader
- Helping Your Child in Math

PERSONAL FINANCE

- Basic Investing
- Investing in Stocks
- Investing in Mutual Funds
- Buying and Selling Your Home
- Plan Your Estate
- Develop a Personal Financial Plan

PHRASE BOOKS

- French
- Spanish
- Italian
- German
- Russian
- Japanese
- Greek

SPORTS FOR KIDS

- Basketball for Kids
- Baseball for Kids
- Hockey for Kids
- Soccer for Kids
- Gymnastics for Kids
- Martial Arts for Kids

**Coles Notes and New Coles Notes are available at the following stores:
Chapters • Coles • Smithbooks • World's Biggest Bookstore**

NOTES & UPDATES